100 Ideas for Secondary Teachers

Teaching Philosophy and Ethics

John L. Taylor

B L O O M S B U R Y

LONDON • NEW DELHI • NEW YORK • SYDNEY

Bloomsbury Education

An imprint of Bloomsbury Publishing Plc

50 Bedford Square
London
WC1B 3DP
UK

1385 Broadway
New York
NY 10018
USA

www.bloomsbury.com

Bloomsbury is a registered trade mark of Bloomsbury Publishing Plc

First published 2014

British Library Cataloguing-in-Publication Data
A catalogue record for this book is available from the British Library.

ISBN: PB: 9781472909565
ePub: 9781472910097
ePDF: 9781472910080

Library of Congress Cataloging-in-Publication Data
A catalog record for this book is available from the Library of Congress.

10 9 8 7 6 5 4 3 2 1

Typeset by Newgen Knowledge Works (P) Ltd., Chennai, India
Printed by CPI Group (UK) Ltd, Croydon, CR0 4YY

This book is produced using paper that is made from wood grown
in managed, sustainable forests. It is natural, renewable and
recyclable. The logging and manufacturing processes conform
to the environmental regulations of the country of origin.

To view more of our titles please visit www.bloomsbury.com

Contents

Acknowledgements

My thanks to the students and colleagues with whom I have worked in developing the ideas in this book. Many of these ideas have been road-tested with my Extended Project and Philosophy students at Rugby School and I am grateful to them for providing many hours of stimulating philosophical conversation: learning philosophy really does happen through dialogue, not monologue. I am also grateful to Robert Abbott, the inventor of the 'Eleusis' game, for permission to make use of this in Idea 13. Particular thanks go to my colleagues Dr Emma Williams, Dr Ralph Levinson and Dr Elizabeth Swinbank, for their suggestions, inspiration and advice and to my wife, Georgina, for being a constant source of wisdom and encouragement.

Introduction

I have always thought of education and philosophy as being essentially connected activities. Both aim to enable deeper understanding and both involve a process of critical, reflective inquiry, in which assumptions are challenged and concepts are clarified. When we are teaching young people, we are not simply filling their heads with factual information: we are developing their minds, challenging them to think more clearly and deeply about ideas, to reflect on the basis of what they are learning, and to consider the implications of new-found knowledge for the rest of life.

In my view, teaching philosophy and ethics to children means actually doing philosophy and ethics with them. It is not about telling students a great long list of facts about the history of ideas from the ancient to the modern world (the 'Plato to NATO' approach). It is about engaging with students in a shared journey of inquiry.

An inquiry-based approach is particularly important when ethical questions are being discussed. It is our job, as philosophical and ethical educators, to provide students with the tools they need to begin thinking for themselves at a richer, deeper level. When dealing with the great unanswered problems of philosophy, it is our job to teach students *how* to think, not *what* to think.

This book provides practical guidance about how to turn these ideals into reality. Some of the ideas relate to philosophy and ethics specifically, while other ideas can be applied in a range of different subject settings, both inside and outside the classroom. Particular emphasis is placed on project work as a vehicle for encouraging philosophical and ethical reflection. The great advantage of project work is that it provides time for students to develop their own ideas, having researched the ideas of others. A combination of exciting classroom discussion, followed by a period of project work, is a great way of helping students to develop their skills as philosophically reflective learners.

How to use this book

This book includes quick, easy, practical ideas for you to dip in and out of, to support you in teaching philosophy and ethics.

Each idea includes:

- A catchy title, easy to refer to and share with your colleagues.
- A quote from a teacher or student describing their experiences of the idea that follows or a problem they may have had that using the idea solves.
- A summary of the idea in bold, making it easy to flick through the book and identify an idea you want to use at a glance.
- A step-by-step guide to implementing the idea.

Each idea also includes one or more of the following:

Teaching tip	Taking it further	Bonus idea ★
Some extra advice on how or how not to run the activity or put the strategy into practice.	Ideas and advice for how to extend the idea or develop it further.	There are 13 bonus ideas in this book that are extra exciting and extra original.

Share how you use these ideas in the classroom and find out what other teachers have done using **#100ideas** and the other hashtags throughout the book.

Starting points

Part 1

Teach philosophically

"Don't just teach philosophy – teach philosophically."

Ever since Socrates, the best teachers of philosophy have taught in a philosophical way. This means engaging students in a process of inquiry into the meaning of words we use every day.

The role model for all teachers of philosophy and ethics is Socrates, the Greek philosopher who earned himself a reputation for niggling away at the bold pronouncements of his fellow Athenians with his probing questions. Socrates' point was that we are all in the dark when it comes to matters of philosophy and ethics, but most of us don't realise this. We talk confidently about knowledge, goodness, truth, God, beauty, freedom, the mind and so on. It is only when we are asked to explain what these words mean that we realise we don't know.

Socratic questioning is a great way to draw students into philosophical inquiry. The purpose is to help them realise that there is a world of fascinating puzzles which opens up as soon as we pause to give attention to words which we use every day, without noticing how mysterious they are.

You know you have hit the mark when students leave the class still arguing. When stimulating students to think independently, nothing is quite so potent as philosophical questions.

Just as a chemical catalyst can speed up a reaction even in small doses, so a droplet or two of philosophy can make your class fizz and sparkle with new ideas and arguments. Consider:

- What makes a good action good?
- What is time?
- Do you have a soul?
- Could there be nothing at all?
- What does the word 'God' mean?

A guided tour of philosophy land

"Help – I'm getting lost!"

Entering the world of philosophy and ethics is a bit like setting sail on a vast ocean for the first time. Providing a map of the major landmarks can help students to find their bearings.

It is easy for students to feel completely lost when they encounter the vast, deep world of philosophical and ethical ideas. It helps if you take them on a short 'guided tour' of the world of philosophy, highlighting the important landmarks (the main thinkers and their ideas) as well as some of the routes which link them.

It is important to avoid overloading the students with information. The aim is not to condense the whole of philosophy and ethics into a few lessons, but simply to give students some sense of the landscape of ideas.

A good way to do this is to tell a series of short stories about influential philosophers. We all respond well to stories; they help to make ideas vivid and memorable. Carefully constructed short stories can illustrate these points:

- What motivates people to do philosophy?
- What questions do philosophers think about?
- How do philosophers answer their questions?
- How is the work of philosophers affected by the world they live in?
- How have philosophers influenced other people, especially other philosophers?

These stories can be told to a group, provided in the form of a short 'story book' of philosophy or, alternatively, you could choose to record them as short podcasts. There are examples of this at the hashtag #storyofphilosophy.

Taking it further

Ask your students to research a particular philosopher then give a presentation describing who the philosopher was and some of the philosopher's main ideas and arguments. This could be done as a short (eight to ten slide) PowerPoint or a poster presentation. If you assign different philosophers to different groups of students, the class as a whole can build up the 'story of philosophy' themselves.

#storyofphilosophy

It's good to talk

"It's when we talk about ideas that we really begin to understand them."

Philosophy and ethics belong to the ongoing conversation about ideas that matter. Discussion with students is the best way of drawing them into this conversation.

Philosophical thinking grows from dialogue. Since philosophy consists of a conversation about ideas, the way to teach it is by drawing students into discussion. Dialogue, not monologue, should be at the heart of the philosophy classroom. Here are some tips about how to get discussion started, and keep it going well:

- Use an attention-grabbing stimulus, such as a weird idea, a disturbing suggestion or an argument for an absurd conclusion to provoke a reaction from your students.
- Don't be scared of letting students argue. The discussion is liveliest when there is disagreement. This is part and parcel of the process of philosophical inquiry.
- Be prepared to play devil's advocate. It is hard to keep the conversation alive if everyone agrees. You may need to take up an opposing position as a way of challenging students to think deeper. Participation in discussion and debate is the foundation for the development of thinking skills.
- Be prepared to move on. Discussions have a natural lifetime. Sometimes they last all lesson, sometimes they fizzle out after a few minutes. Have a follow-up stimulus question or activity up your sleeve in case this happens.

Flipped philosophy

"We learn more when we know a bit about what we are going to be talking about."

Philosophical discussions work best when those taking part in them have learnt a bit about the topic beforehand. If students have some prior knowledge, then everyone is ready to engage in an analysis of this knowledge.

The idea of the 'flipped classroom' has become popular in recent years, but the idea itself is an old one, enshrined in the language of traditional schools which set 'prep' (preparation): work done before the lesson to ensure that the student has some background knowledge in place before the lesson begins.

This is a good technique if your aim is to help students develop their thinking skills and their analytical abilities through discussion. If they have done some prior reading, they will have something to bring to the discussion, and instead of having to ensure that they acquire all the information they need, you will be able to move the discussion on to analyse ideas and evaluate arguments.

For this to work effectively you need to make sure that the class understands the point of the exercise. If they feel that it is your job to 'tell them exactly what they need to know' they may not appreciate the importance of individual study ahead of a lesson. You don't need to set a great deal of prep: what matters is that the material you choose is a good starting point for discussion.

What if some students don't complete their prep? To anticipate this, you could ask them to produce and hand in study notes, which you can check before you move to a whole-class discussion.

Teaching tip

A good philosophical discussion can often focus on a single argument (for example, the first cause cosmological argument). Ask students to read a brief account of the argument and research common criticisms. In the discussion, you can then focus on exploring the logic of the argument.

Taking it further

Asking students to present to the class will help keep them on their toes. Ask one of them to introduce a discussion by presenting what they have learnt from their background reading.

The power of podcasts

"Short, snappy talks on important topics are a versatile resource."

Since philosophy begins with conversation, it makes sense to use audio files such as short podcast talks and interviews to carry the learning process forward.

Now that it is so easy to create recordings of people talking about philosophy, as well as to access a rich supply of other people's recordings, philosophical teachers have a fantastic resource at their disposal. Various formats work well:

- Short recordings of yourself explaining a key idea or argument.
- A discussion with another teacher, exploring an argument through dialogue.
- Interviews with students to elicit their ideas as a stimulus.
- *Vox pop* interviews with people as a source of ideas for discussion.
- Excerpts of recordings of class debates.

Create your own podcasts using the Windows sound recorder program. Here are some tips to create high-quality recordings:

- Use a good quality pair of headphones with a microphone attached (the Microsoft lifechat headphones are very good).
- Script recordings beforehand.
- Get the audio settings right on the computer (turn off the internal mic).
- Import your recording into iTunes to turn it into an MP3 file.
- You can also record a voiceover for a PowerPoint. Click on slide show, record narration, and use a reasonable quality level (16 bit mono or stereo works fine).

There are some excellent online podcasts to be found at #philosophypodcasts.

#philosophypodcasts

Easy reading

"Keep it simple, especially to start with."

Students can find philosophical and ethical texts really challenging to read, especially when they are starting out. Finding ways to make the texts as easy to read as possible will help encourage them.

I can still remember how utterly bewildering it felt to read philosophical articles for the first time. The complexity and depth of the ideas and the fact that philosophical and ethical ideas need to be understood as part of an ongoing exchange of arguments can create a barrier which discourages students from reading them.

To help students with this challenging but vital task, think about how you can make it as easy as possible for them to begin reading philosophy.

Given the importance of knowing some of the context within which a philosopher is working, it can help if you set the scene. Tell students a little about the philosopher, their main concerns, the era in which they were working, and with whom they were arguing.

Often, it makes sense to begin by giving students a summary from a good secondary source, such as an introductory philosophy guide or a good textbook, before letting them loose on the writings of the philosopher.

When you are reading primary source material, remember that philosophical and ethical writing is frequently quite dense, so don't expect students to read huge amounts at a time. A good way of breaking up text is to isolate specific arguments, which can often be just one or two paragraphs long, and focus on a close reading of these.

Teaching tip

It is always wise to link reading to some form of other activity, whether note-taking, answering comprehension questions, or class discussion, which will help you gauge the level of understanding that students have developed.

Taking it further

When students are ready to read some primary sources, point them to www.earlymoderntexts.com. This is a terrific compilation of philosophical works, lightly edited to make them as easy to read as possible.

Going off-piste

"The lessons I remember best are the ones when we just talked about ideas."

Just occasionally, it is a good idea to put the plans aside and simply let the conversation flow.

I once had the chance to teach philosophy to a group of students with no syllabus, no learning outcomes and no formal assessment at all. One of these students later told me he had learnt more from those lessons than any others.

Unstructured, free, open exploration of ideas, where you forget about sticking to the syllabus and simply go where the discussion leads, can result in some of the most exciting, memorable – and at times, deepest – discussions of all.

Of course you can't do this in every lesson. But sometimes, going 'off-piste' can add real depth and meaning to the learning process. This is especially true when the conversation turns to the deepest questions of all – about God, values, and the meaning and purpose of life. What is philosophy for, if not for exploring these questions?

Allowing such free discussion shows students that beyond the formalities of learning outcomes, assessment objectives and set texts, philosophy is a living, breathing, ongoing exploration of life itself, at the deepest, most personal level.

Critics may say that these free-flowing conversations are a waste of valuable curriculum time, but they can refresh and revitalise the learning process. Going off-piste once in a while means that when you come back to the formal stuff, students feel more alive and ready to engage in their studies once again.

Ask a funny question

"That's a really interesting question!"

Philosophical questions have tremendous power to stimulate curiosity and so get the process of inquiry started.

Philosophy has a reputation of being a dry, abstract, rather pointless subject, offering nothing more than endless questions and providing few answers. Added to this, many students simply don't know what the subject is all about. Therefore, an important part of the role of teaching philosophy and ethics is, bluntly, marketing it. How do we go about hooking students on philosophy?

One of the best ways of stimulating students' interest is by asking questions. Great novel writers or film-makers can draw you in by inventing magical, enchanted worlds. Philosophy has the power to make the world itself seem strange, magical and surprising.

I am always looking out for opportunities to ask students questions which will make them stop and realise that some fascinating philosophical puzzles lie just beneath the surface of the everyday world.

This can often happen outside the classroom. Over lunch, for example, I might ask a student how they know the table they are sitting at really exists.

The best questions to ask are ones that students themselves might have thought of and are likely to find interesting. The question 'Is my blue the same as yours?' is a good one and so are questions about personal identity ('Are you the same person today as you were yesterday?').

> **Teaching tip**
>
> At the same time as using questions to hook students on philosophy, watch out that you don't lead them to think that philosophers do nothing but ask questions, or that anyone's answer is as good as anyone else's. Questions are the way into philosophy – and once inside, there's a lot to learn about which answers are better than others.

Modelling thinking

"The best way to teach philosophy to students is to do philosophy with students."

If you want students to learn to think philosophically, you need to let them see how you think your way through a problem.

Teaching tip

Philosophical inquiry is exciting but can seem confusing and even pointless, especially when students expect their teacher to just 'tell them the answers', rather than explore problems where the answers may not be known. Explain that the point of inquiry-based lessons is for students to learn how to do something, namely how to explore a philosophical problem, rather than simply learning a set of 'right' answers.

Aristotle once said that we learn how to build or play music by doing these things. The same applies to learning philosophy and ethics. We learn to think by thinking, and nothing is more valuable when we are starting out than having a good role model. Part of the job of the philosophy teacher is to model the art of philosophical thinking.

This does not mean that students should be learning to parrot your ideas. They should reach their own conclusions, but they should learn to get there using logical argument and careful analysis of concepts, which they can pick up from you by the process of 'mimesis' (imitation).

Philosophy classes should include periods in which you and the students work together on a philosophical or ethical problem. In Plato's dialogues, you will find that this was how Socrates worked: he pursued truth in the company of his students and they in turn learnt what it meant to apply philosophical methods to a problem.

This sort of joint inquiry can happen quite naturally in response to questions students raise. Students often raise issues which are a bit 'off-topic', but by taking the class off in new, unexpected and unexplored directions, you can show students how you think your way through a problem, and they can learn from seeing the process of philosophical inquiry in action.

The philosophical classroom

"Create space for thought."

It is worth thinking about what you can do to turn your classroom into a space which stimulates thought and encourages reflection.

Your main task as a teacher of philosophy and ethics is to stimulate your students to think for themselves. The way you use the space in your classroom can help to create an environment which is conducive to thought. Here are some tips:

- Fill the walls with posters with thought-provoking quotations from the great philosophers. It is good if you can juxtapose contrasting ideas: for example, 'God is dead', (Nietzsche) next to 'God is that than which nothing greater can be conceived' (Anselm) or use provocative sayings, for example, 'Most people would sooner die than think, and most people do' (Bertrand Russell).
- Invite your group to create a sequence of posters to illustrate aspects of a particular topic, or, if funds allow, buy some professionally printed images.
- Philosophy is all about argument. Create an argument wall, where you can start an argument, and students can add their own responses. Change the argument on a regular basis.
- If students have produced project work or extended essays on philosophical ideas, get these nicely printed, bound and put on display. This helps to send the message that their ideas really do matter and encourages other students to read and learn from the thoughts of their peers.

Teaching tip

People often say that philosophy is an abstract subject with little relevance to everyday life. Nothing could be further from the truth. Look out for newspaper stories or online articles which raise philosophical and ethical questions about society, belief, values, the future of technology and so on. Displaying these is a way of reminding students that life itself is constantly presenting us with philosophical challenges.

The value of philosophy

"It's surprising how useful philosophy can be."

You need to market philosophy to students, and one way to do this is to remind them of the value of the skills that you can acquire through learning philosophy.

Teaching tip

You should give students some idea of what philosophy is. Explain that it is the study of ultimate questions, such as: Is there a God? Do we have free will? Do we know that physical objects exist? Is the mind the same as the brain? Is there an objective difference between good and bad acts?

When students are thinking about options choices, part of the process is informing them about the benefits of choosing a subject. So how do you explain the value of philosophy?

Ask what people such as Ricky Gervais, David Cameron, former *Blue Peter* presenter Liz Barker and former England cricket captain Mike Brearley have in common. The answer is that they all studied philosophy.

This shows that philosophy can be useful in all sorts of different walks of life. This is an important point to make because students may find themselves interested in the questions of philosophy and ethics, but doubtful as to whether studying these further will be 'worth it' (that's to say, likely to help them get a job in the future).

Tell students that it is worth studying philosophy because of the valuable skills they can gain (for example, analytical skills, logical thinking, presenting and criticising arguments and thinking outside the box). It is also worthwhile because life and work will require them to think about questions for which there is no known answer and philosophy provides them with tools to begin doing this.

Dual-purpose lessons

"You don't have to choose between teaching skills and teaching knowledge – you can do both!"

With a little careful planning, you can teach lessons which develop thinking skills and provide information about topics at the same time.

There is a long-running debate about whether we should focus on teaching skills or teaching knowledge. But it is possible to plan lessons which do both. Some topics naturally lend themselves to activities which in turn develop particular skills. So when you are planning a sequence of lessons, think about which skills you expect students to develop, then decide which topics provide the best context for developing these. The result will be a 'dual-purpose' lesson, in which the objectives include acquisition of knowledge and skills. Here are some examples:

- If you are teaching a topic in which there are a number of standard arguments (for example, the existence of God, arguments for mind-body dualism), read extracts from philosophers in which arguments are stated. Then ask students to restate the argument in their own words. In this way, they learn the arguments as well as how to begin argument analysis.
- On a topic such as euthanasia, ask students to find a newspaper opinion piece, or an online article, containing arguments for euthanasia and one containing arguments against. Students can then be asked to make a list of specific arguments on both sides. This activity teaches the importance of identifying arguments and counter-arguments.

Teaching tip

Studying arguments for and against the existence of God provides a good context for teaching students about the logical structure of argument. Provide students with a sample argument (William Lane Craig's Kalam cosmological argument works well here). Then ask them to identify the premises and the conclusion of the argument. They can consider whether the premises are true and, if so, whether the conclusion follows. This is a helpful technique for developing the skill of precise, focused critical evaluation of argument.

Stimulating inquiry

Part 2

Eleusis

"It's amazing how much you can learn when you are having fun!"

A game which explores how we reason is a great way of introducing students to the study of logic.

Games are a terrific way of enlivening lessons and also anchoring key ideas in the student's mind. One of my favourites is a game called 'Eleusis', invented by Robert Abbott to illustrate the nature of inductive reasoning. For further details, see the inventor's website: www. logicmazes.com/games/eleusis.

You will need several packs of cards. Divide students into groups of between two and four. One person in each group is the 'rule-maker'. It is their job to invent a rule (for example, 'red cards must be followed by black cards' or 'only even numbered cards are allowed').

The cards are turned over one-by-one. Cards that fit the rule are placed in one row, cards which don't fit are placed in a row below. The rest of the group have to work out what the rule is by looking at the rows of upturned cards.

Stop the group after a few rounds and discuss what it can tell us about reasoning processes. At the heart of the game is Hume's 'problem of induction': how ever many cards are turned over, the pattern could always fit with more than one rule. It is impossible to prove a general rule from any finite set of data. This can lead into a discussion of scepticism and knowledge: Do we know that our theories are true? Can a scientific theory ever be proven? Can a theory about the meaning of a novel or a historical document ever be proven true, or is it always possible that there is an alternative, equally good theory?

Taking it further

Eleusis can also be used to explore issues about the psychology of theory creation: How do we come to form theories? Is it pure guesswork or are we guided by patterns we partially recognise? Another point for exploration is the use of counter-examples to disprove hypotheses. We may never be able to prove a general rule, but it only takes a single piece of data to disprove it. It is often said that in science, it is never possible to prove a hypothesis, only to disprove it. Is the same true in philosophy?

Experimental philosophy

"It's fascinating finding out how my mind works."

Activities that tell students something about the way their mind works provide an intriguing starting point for discussion.

Aristotle taught that it is a good idea to look at what people actually think about philosophical issues when starting out on an inquiry. In recent years, so-called 'experimental philosophy' has grown more sophisticated, with full-scale surveys designed to gather data about people's philosophical intuitions on moral issues and questions about the nature and limits of reason.

One way into such discussion is to ask students to try activities such as the Wason selection test, which reveals surprising things about biases in our thought processes. The website www.philosophyexperiments.com gives students an opportunity to try out such tests.

These activities can lead into a discussion of what this tells us about our rational, logical nature and its limits. Philosophers such as Hume argue that since human reason is fallible, we should be cautious about the conclusions we draw in philosophy and ethics. Does the evidence from experimental philosophy support Hume?

Moral philosophy is another context in which experimental philosophy can be usefully applied. Professor Michael Sandel's 'Justice at Harvard' lecture series (www.justiceharvard.org) begins with a sequence of hypothetical scenarios which have become quite famous as starting points for inquiry into the foundations of ethics: the 'trolley' thought experiments.

Teaching tip

Remind students that the fact that many people think a certain way does not imply that they are right. A majority of people in the UK may favour the return of capital punishment, but this does not prove that this would be the right thing to do. Using survey techniques to gather data is a good starting point for philosophical inquiry, but take care that students understand that this data cannot be used to prove a philosophical idea.

Taking it further

Watch ten minutes of Michael Sandel's first lecture, then stop to ask your class for their responses as questions are posed. This will take you straight to the heart of the debate about the adequacy of consequentialist ethics

Uncovering mystery

"Philosophy makes the ordinary world seem extraordinary."

To the philosophical eye, there is nothing ordinary about the world around us. Even an obvious statement such as 'grass is green' turns out to be full of philosophical mystery when you look into it.

Philosophy is the quest for a deeper understanding of concepts that we use every day without realising how intricate, deep and complex they really are. One good way of showing students how language is a rich source of philosophical mystery is to take an obvious statement such as 'grass is green' and pull a host of philosophical puzzles out of it. Questions which provide a good way into this topic include:

- Should we say 'grass is green' or rather 'grass looks green'?
- Does the fact that grass doesn't look green at night mean it isn't truly green?
- If dogs or aliens can't see the green colour of grass, does this mean it isn't really there?
- If grass is made of atoms, and atoms have no colour, does this mean grass has no colour?
- Is the greenness of grass really a quality of an idea in the mind, not a quality of objects in the physical world?

The philosophical issue lying behind these questions is that of the distinction between appearance and reality. You may need to explain to students that the point of the exercise is not to turn them into out-and-out sceptics, who believe nothing, but to show them how questioning and analysing concepts can lead to a deeper understanding. Grass may really be green – but what do we mean when we say this?

Taking it further

Debates about what is objectively real occur throughout philosophy. It is often argued that since science cannot tell us the difference between right and wrong, morality must be subjective. Is this argument any better than the argument that denies the reality of qualities such as colour? There is a podcast at #philosophypodcasts that explores this.

The method of doubt

"When it comes to philosophy, faith is not necessarily a virtue and doubt has its benefits."

The method of doubt is a valuable tool when it comes to searching for the truth.

In a religious context, faith is spoken of as a virtue and doubt tends to be frowned upon. But as Descartes showed when he employed the 'method of doubt' as a tool in the search for truth, doubt is not necessarily a bad thing.

The point is to use sceptical questioning to dig down to the foundations and find out if a belief is based on solid grounds. The method of doubt involves asking questions such as:

- Why did you say that?
- What makes you think that is true?
- What is your evidence for that statement?
- Do you know that or is it just something you believe?
- Can you really be sure about that?

When confronted with sustained questioning of their ideas and beliefs, students may complain that all philosophers do is ask questions and make everything doubtful. A good answer to this objection was provided by Hume, who distinguished between 'excessive' and 'mitigated' scepticism. Excessive scepticism involves questioning everything, with the result that a paralysing lack of activity ensues. Total scepticism makes life impossible. But mitigated scepticism involves exploring the limits of our knowledge, with the aim of focusing our attention on what we can know, and putting aside fruitless debates about what is beyond our understanding. It is worth explaining this distinction to help students distinguish between fertile and sterile ways of using doubt.

Taking it further

Ask students to reflect on how science, philosophy, history, theology and so on all make use of 'mitigated scepticism' in the search for truth. For Hume's account of mitigated scepticism, see Chapter 12 of *An Enquiry concerning Human Understanding*, at www.davidhume.org.

Paradox play

"This is making my head hurt!"

Paradoxes are an effective stimulus to philosophical thinking.

Teaching tip

When discussing the Achilles and the tortoise paradox, students frequently argue that it seems obvious that Achilles will win the race. You will need to explain that while this seems true, the paradox arises because there also appears to be a sound logical argument for saying he cannot.

Much philosophical discussion begins with paradox, when we find ourselves confronted by two statements, both of which seem reasonable, but which apparently contradict each other. Putting paradoxes in front of students is an effective way of getting philosophical discussion and debate going. In the process, students can begin to appreciate valuable lessons about the philosophically puzzling nature of concepts such as number, space, time or truth. Here are some examples you can use in the classroom:

- The liar paradox: Give students a piece of paper with the statement 'This sentence is false'.
- The double-liar paradox: Give students a piece of paper, on one side of which is the statement 'The statement on the other side of this paper is false', and on the other 'The statement on the other side of this paper is true'.
- The time traveller paradox: If you could make a time machine and travel back in time, it would be possible to kill your own grandfather. But then, you would never have been born...
- Zeno's paradoxes. The simplest is the 'arrow': before an arrow can cross the room, it has to cross half the room, before it can cross half the room, it must cross a quarter of the room, and so infinitely on. So the arrow can only move if it can cross an infinite number of regions of space. (For an entertaining presentation of the Achilles and the tortoise paradox, see www.youtube.com/watch?v=skM37PcZmWE.)

Paradoxes sometimes infuriate students and leave them wondering if there is any point thinking about them. You can draw out two possible conclusions. One is that reality is paradoxical: our best attempts to think about it are bound to lead to apparent contradiction. A more optimistic moral is that the presence of paradox shows that our assumptions need to be questioned. For example, the liar paradoxes assume that the sentences on the pages are either true or false and Zeno's paradoxes assume that space and time are infinitely divisible. Perhaps we can find a way ahead through questioning our assumptions.

Taking it further

The topic of infinity is a rich source of paradox. Ask students to carry out some research to find some of the 'paradoxes of the infinite'. This can form a starting point for a class discussion of the question of whether anything could be infinite.

Bonus idea ★

Ask students whether it would be fair for a maths teacher to ask them to write down the whole of Pi for homework. This is a way of exploring the question of whether an infinite series of tasks could be completed – a central issue in Zeno's paradoxes. It is hard to conceive of how an infinite series could be completed in a finite period of time, and it isn't clear whether it could be completed even in infinite time.

Making philosophy real

"Everyday life is a rich resource for philosophical thought."

One of the best ways of drawing students into philosophical inquiry is to begin with questions that arise from everyday life.

Taking it further

For discussion of Cartesian dualism, see www.closertotruth.com.

Debates about whether we know the physical world exists can be fun, but they can also leave students feeling that philosophical scepticism is irrelevant to real life. Worrying that life might be just a dream probably doesn't keep many people awake at night. Here are some real-world contexts which raise genuine sceptical concerns.

Ghosts: In my experience, in most groups of students, at least one person will have a good ghost story to share. This is an ideal starting point for discussion about perception, knowledge, doubt, experience and the paranormal. What possible explanations are there for paranormal experiences? How should we determine their most likely cause?

Complementary medicine: Once again, in a typical class, at least one student will have had experience of using complementary therapies such as homeopathy. Is there evidence that such therapies are effective? Could this be due to placebo effect? Why are some therapies called 'mainstream' and others 'complementary'?

Bonus idea ★

The topic of magic provides a good starting point for a discussion of the distinction between appearance and reality. A conjuror exploits the fact that we tend to believe what our senses tell us, even when we know, at some level, that what we are seeing can't really be happening. For an interesting exploration of the psychology of illusion, see this interview with Derren Brown: www. youtube.com/watch?v= U1cMmz7m3AA.

Angels: Many people believe in the existence of guiding spiritual beings. As well as the question about the evidential basis for this belief, there is an interesting philosophical issue about the concept of the supernatural. Could non-physical agents interact with the physical world? The problem of 'interaction' is often posed in connection with Cartesian dualism, but it has a wider application.

Dream time

"Have you ever had a dream that was so real, you couldn't tell it was just a dream?"

Talking about dreams is a good way of exploring the issue of the gap between the way things are and the way they seem to be.

In Idea 18, I wrote that few people are likely to stay awake worrying about whether they are dreaming. But what about people who suffer from vivid dreams: dreams that are so lifelike that it is impossible to tell the difference between them and the experiences we have when awake? If you can't tell whether you are awake or dreaming, how can you know whether the things around you are real?

Talking about dreams is a good way into discussion of the problem of knowledge, since it links to an experience many students will have had – of mistakenly thinking something was happening, only to awake and find they had dreamed it. Discussion of this topic can lead into a number of interesting areas.

- Can we ever know for sure that what our senses appear to be telling us is in fact true? What signs distinguish dreaming from wakefulness?
- According to the song *Row, row, row your boat,* 'Life is but a dream', an idea we can also find in Plato, according to whom the world we encounter through sense perception is largely an illusory one. Is Plato right? If our senses cannot be trusted, how can we have knowledge of reality?
- How should we describe dreams? Is having a dream like watching a movie in the privacy of your own mind? (The analogy between dreams and movies is helpfully explored by Colin McGinn in his book *The Power of Movies.*)

Teaching tip

Do dreams tell us anything about ourselves? According to Freud, dreams should be understood as expressions of unconscious desires. This is a psychological theory, but it can also be explored philosophically. Does it make sense to talk about an 'unconscious' desire?

Taking it further

Discuss the role of dreams in literature (for example, in *Alice in Wonderland* or *A Midsummer Night's Dream*) and also in the movies (in films such as *Vanilla Sky*).

23

Philosophy in the movies

"Some films really do bring philosophical ideas to life."

Asking students to identify and discuss the philosophical ideas explored in a movie is a good way of developing their analytical skills.

Part of the enjoyment of a movie is 'switching off' – entering into the world it depicts without analysing it critically. But some films do such a good job of opening up deep and interesting philosophical and ethical questions that our critical faculties are jolted awake. Films like this can be a great classroom resource, helping to make philosophical ideas stand out in fresh and exciting ways.

Many of the 'big questions' of philosophy can be approached this way. A good technique is to watch a clip, then ask some open questions ('What do you think the film was about?', 'Was there any philosophy in that film, would you say?') which will encourage students to start reflecting and, hopefully, identify philosophical elements within the story. Here are a few suggestions, though there are many other films that you could use:

- *The Matrix* is a classic for exploring the problem of knowledge of the external world.
- *Back to the Future* brings some of the paradoxes of time travel into focus.
- *Minority Report* raises issues such as fatalism, free will and determinism.

Taking it further

Ask students to write a 'philosophical film review' of a favourite movie of theirs. Asking students to identify and explain philosophical issues within a specific context is a good way of helping them develop their philosophical understanding.

A web of illusion

"Is seeing really believing?"

Optical illusions provide a good way of stimulating students to think about the reliability of sense perception.

Sometimes the subject of philosophy comes up with students outside the classroom. Since most students have no idea what it is all about, I like to find specific examples of philosophical problems for them to think about. The argument from illusion is a good one to use. I might draw two parallel lines of the same length, ask the students to verify that they are the same length, then add diagonals to form a Muller-Lyer image, like this:

Now, the two horizontal lines of the same length look different lengths. How is that possible? What does this mean about how we see reality? We normally rely on our senses, but if our senses can deceive us, can we ever know what the world is like?

What is philosophically interesting about illusions is that they show us that perception isn't always as simple as just finding out about the world by looking at it. There is a difference between the way things are and the way they appear to be. Just how big is this gap? Can it ever be fully closed? How can we tell the difference between the cases in which our senses are reliable and those in which they are not?

Teaching tip

If you are exploring the topic of illusion in the classroom, you could use various other good sources of images and films:

- Michael Bach's optical illusions website: www.michaelbach.de/ot.
- Illusion of the year 2014: www.illusionoftheyear.com/cat/top-10-finalists/2014.
- Dan Dennett on the illusion of consciousness: www.youtube.com/watch?v=fjbWr3ODbAo.

Philosophical pictures

"Does what we think change what we see?"

Images which can be seen in different ways can be used to explore the question of how what we see is affected by what we think.

Is there an objective world which exists independently of our minds or do our minds shape, or even create, reality for us? This question takes us right to the heart of many philosophical problems. An effective way of introducing it in the classroom is through the use of 'Gestalt' images: images which can be seen as one thing or another. You can find a collection by entering 'Gestalt' into Google images.

How an image such as the 'duck/rabbit' or the 'old woman/young woman' is seen can vary depending on the thoughts of the perceiver, a phenomenon known as 'aspect perception'. In some cases, as with the 'face on the mountainside', until you are told what to look for it is hard to see the image at all.

Questions worth discussing here include:

- To what extent do we see the things we expect to see?
- Is it only possible to see something for which you already have a concept?
- Is what we see something which exists outside the mind, or is it something which the mind creates or shapes?
- Does the phenomenon of 'aspect perception' help to explain how religious experiences are shaped by cultural forces?

Taking it further

Philosophers of science such as RN Hanson and Thomas Kuhn argued that perception is 'theory-laden' and thus we must revise the traditional image of science as a purely objective process of testing theories against observation. It is worth discussing whether this account of science is more realistic than the traditional view, or whether it makes scientific knowledge too subjective.

Experimenting with thought

"I love the way philosophy explores the limits of what can be imagined."

Thought experiments provide a stimulating starting point for exploring philosophical topics.

In the history of philosophy, the technique of constructing imaginary scenarios to test what can be conceived, or to challenge us to think differently about what seems obvious, has been used to good effect on many occasions. One merit of this approach is that it employs stories and images; these are more concrete and vivid than abstract theories or logical arguments.

This doesn't mean that the arguments don't matter. The best thought experiments are those which lead into a discussion. The thought experiment should not be so far-fetched that it can teach us little about the real world: a discussion about whether a computer could think is likely to be more productive than one about the possibility of intelligent stones. Some of the most productive thought experiments are those which have been linked to scientific investigation (for example, Galileo's story about dropping a light and a heavy ball from the leaning tower of Pisa).

Consider these thought experiments to stimulate discussion and argument:

- Could you exist outside your body? Does it make sense to conceive of yourself as a pure, disembodied mind?
- Could other people be 'philosophical zombies', who act and behave just as you do, but lack any internal conscious mental states?
- Suppose we replaced each neurone in your brain with a silicon chip that functioned in the same way ... would you still have a mind?

Teaching tip

Use a thought experiment as a starting point for a discussion, but be ready to move the discussion on to an exploration of the underlying philosophical issues. For example, discussion of 'out-of-body' experiences should lead into a discussion of arguments for and against mind–body dualism.

Possible worlds

"Imagine if the world was like this ...."

Talking about possible worlds can be helpful when explaining philosophical theories.

Talking about possible worlds is a way of exploring how the world might be, and it can be very useful when exploring particular philosophical topics. Here are some cases where it can be useful:

- To illustrate the idea of logical necessity, explain to students that there are no possible worlds in which squares are five-sided: however the world is, squares must have four sides.
- To explore the question of whether God necessarily exists, ask students whether they think that God exists in some possible worlds, and not others.
- To explore sceptical arguments, ask students to imagine a possible world in which they have the same experiences they do now, but as a result of being connected to a powerful computer, programmed to deceive them (as in *The Matrix*). How could we ever tell we are not in this world?
- Explain Hume's problem of induction by asking students to imagine world B, which is just like the normal world up until midnight tonight – but after midnight, things in world B go crazy: pigs start to fly, the sun vanishes etc. How do we know we do not live in world B?

Real-world thought experiments

"Sometimes truth is stranger than fiction."

Real case studies can work as well as fantasy tales for stimulating philosophical discussion.

Thought experiments sometimes strike students as so far-fetched as to be not worth discussion. So it is worth being ready with a few examples of genuine case studies which can be equally compelling as starting points for philosophical inquiry. These show that philosophical questions about topics such as consciousness, personal identity, or the basis of religious experience belong to the real world.

A combination of a thought experiment, backed up with some description of real-world case studies, can be very effective.

- Could consciousness exist in unconscious people? Cambridge scientists found that brain scans of a patient in a 'persistent vegetative state' provide evidence that he could answer questions even while apparently unconscious.
- Could free will be an illusion? Benjamin Libet found evidence which seems to suggest that the brain has 'chosen in advance' how to act, even in the case of apparently free choices.
- Could personal identity exist without long-term memory? There are cases of people whose memories reach back in time no more than a few seconds.
- Could religious experience be just a brain process? Michael Persinger claims to be able to create religious experiences by magnetic stimulation of particular regions of the brain.

Taking it further

Links to video clips introducing some of these topics can be found at the hashtag below. It is important that students realise that these stories provide us with data to be explained – they are not 'proofs' of particular philosophical theories, since more than one interpretation can be given for each of them. For example – perhaps a religious believer would reply to Persinger that God creates religious experience by means of brain processes.

#realworldphilosophy

29

The power of stories

"Everybody loves a story."

Telling a story is a great way of making an abstract argument concrete and memorable.

Arthur Schopenhauer noted the way that we respond much more to concrete examples than to abstract argument. Finding a story which makes a philosophical point is an effective way of making arguments more memorable.

For example, I often introduce the materialist theory of the mind by telling the story of Phineas Gage, a railway worker in America who, in 1848, experienced a horrendous injury when an explosion blew a metal rod straight through his head. Remarkably, not only did he survive but he was reported to be conscious only minutes later. However, his personality was dramatically altered as a result, so much so that he scarcely seemed to be the same person. Gage's story is significant since it provides evidence of the close dependence of mental processes on brain function. Introducing the topic of the mind–body problem by means of stories like this adds interest and reality to the philosophical discussion.

Consider these philosophically interesting stories:

- Philosophers such as Plato make use of stories such as the 'Cave analogy' to make philosophical points.
- Philosophical fiction such as *The Time Machine*, *Charlotte's Web* or *The Brothers Karamazov* can be used as starting points for philosophical inquiry.
- There are stories which have been written specifically to introduce philosophy (for example, *Sophie's World*, *Harry Stottlemeier's Discovery*).

From story to argument

"OK – now let's think through the logic of the arguments within the story we've just heard."

Having introduced a philosophical issue by means of a story, it is worth taking time to explore the detailed logic of the arguments contained within it.

Philosophy is not just about interesting and unusual stories – it is about the critical assessment of the logical validity of arguments. Teasing out the arguments contained within a story is a philosophical exercise in its own right and it is something that needs to be done before the arguments can be evaluated. We need to know exactly what the argument is before we can evaluate whether it is any good. Philosophical inquiry usually involves three steps:

- Introduce the philosophical stimulus (the story, case study or thought experiment).
- Take time to identify and lay out the philosophical arguments within the stimulus material as carefully as possible.
- Evaluate these arguments.

So, for example, you could introduce the problem of personal identity by using an argument from Derek Parfit based on the idea of teletransportation. Suppose you stepped into a teletransporter and stepped out on Mars, but then you are told that the original version of you on Earth did not dematerialise. What should we now say? Are you really on Mars, on Earth, both, or neither? Each of these conclusions can be defended.

There is a logical argument within this story which is designed to show that there are cases in which there is no correct answer to questions about personal identity.

Teaching tip

This argument relies on the use of a thought experiment. Some students might think it is therefore too unrealistic. But there are other stories about personal identity which raise similar problems. For some examples, see Julian Baggini's book *The Ego Trick*.

Taking it further

For resources to explore the topic of personal identity further, look at some of the links available at the hashtag below.

#philosophyof
personalidentity

Genealogical explanation

"Let's have a look at where this problem came from."

Explaining the historical background to a philosophical problem gives us richer ways of thinking about it.

To understand a complex idea in philosophy it helps to know something about its history. An understanding of history can illuminate the present and, in the case of ideas, can help to suggest new ways of thinking which might otherwise have been ignored within contemporary discussions. This is the idea behind 'genealogical explanation'.

For example, when discussing the ethics of animal welfare, it helps if students understand the history of ideas about the relationship between human and non-human animals. Traditionally, the Christian doctrine of human uniqueness (that man is uniquely made in the image of God) was used to argue for an anthropocentric approach to ethics, in which humanity has rights (and responsibilities) which other species do not.

In the modern era, this conception of ethics began to be questioned. This came about at a time when the Christian foundations of ethics were themselves being challenged by the arguments of Enlightenment philosophers. The development of Darwinian evolution, with its central idea of the 'tree of life' and the inter-relatedness of all species, gave further impetus to this questioning.

As even this cursory sketch shows, the contemporary discussion of the ethics of our treatment of animals has been shaped by important currents in the history of ideas, with influences coming from science, philosophy and theology.

Everyday ethics

"Life itself offers a rich source of ethical puzzles."

The best way to engage students in ethical discussion is to begin with issues that matter to them.

Since ethics concerns matters of value, and of how we ought to act, it is inescapably part of the whole of life. It follows that more or less any topic has an ethical aspect, and that with a little imagination we can introduce students to philosophical ethics by means of case studies which draw on issues that interest them and about which they are likely to have views of their own.

For example, a topic likely to grab the interest of teenage boys is football. With a little guidance, a debate about the justifiability of paying extremely large transfer fees to footballers can be used to open up important meta-ethical issues. If someone feels that a transfer fee is 'wrong', what is the basis for this? What makes us believe that a fee is excessive? What is the standard? In general, should footballer's pay be subject to some ethical constraints, or is it simply a matter of letting the market decide?

Discussion of this topic may lead into the more general question of what makes any action right or wrong – and with this, we are right at the heart of ethics.

A simple way to structure the discussion is to ask for arguments for and against the proposition that footballers are paid too much. Then take a step back, and look at the ethical assumptions which are being made. For example, if it is argued that the pay is too high because they 'don't deserve it' – well, what makes a wage fair?

> **Teaching tip**
>
> Watch out for the shoulder-shrugging relativist, who dismisses ethical discussion with the conversation-stopping 'well, it's just a matter of opinion isn't it'. You might reply by asking whether they would agree that left-handed students should be set less homework. More generally, the issue here is one about the possibility of having a reasoned discussion – and here the proof of the pudding is in the eating. Even relativists will feel the need to give some reasons for their views, if the topic is one that actually matters to them. This is another reason why it can be valuable to begin ethical discussions with topics that students care about.

From ordinary life to metaphysics

"Metaphysics is all about the biggest questions of all."

The way to draw students into metaphysics is to show them how to inquire into the meaning of their own conceptual scheme.

Metaphysics has had a chequered history in philosophy. Originally it formed one of the central branches of the discipline, being seen as inquiry into the fundamental nature of reality, yet in the era of logical positivism it came to be discarded as meaningless. More recently still, metaphysics has had something of a revival, though suspicion about the credentials of the enterprise remains, and many philosophers prefer to base their metaphysics as squarely as possible on the findings of natural science.

In the classroom, a helpful approach is to employ Sir Peter Strawson's idea of 'descriptive metaphysics', by which he meant inquiry into the concepts which we ordinarily use, unreflectively, in all our thought about the world. This idea has the merit of starting with something we know about – namely, how we think and speak – and avoiding too much idle speculation.

One way of introducing students to descriptive metaphysics is to ask them to make a list of abstract, general words – for example, 'God', 'soul', 'free will', 'identity', 'mind', 'number' and so forth. Then explore what these words mean and how they come to have a meaning.

Some people say that this approach means that philosophy is just a matter of playing with words. But it could be said that a philosophical inquiry into the meaning of the word 'mind' is a way of exploring what the mind really is.

One point you could make is that we define some words by pointing to examples (for example, chair, table, red). But we can't define abstract terms in this way. So how do they get their meaning?

A helpful answer is provided by Wittgenstein: what fixes the meaning of a word is the way it is used. So having identified some metaphysical words, ask students for some sentences in which they are used, and then explore how the word functions to give meaning to the sentence. Of course, one thing that might emerge is that many of these words are hard to define – and some, the sceptic might argue, are without any fixed meaning.

Taking it further

Invite students to think about what philosophical problems are. Some philosophers would say that philosophical problems reflect the fact that we become confused about the way language works. Others would say that metaphysics involves an inquiry into the fundamental structure of reality. Is either view more plausible?

Bonus idea ★

Discussion of metaphysics can lead naturally into the question of the link between science and philosophy. Ask your class to carry out research in preparation for a debate on the motion that science has taken over from philosophy. A good place to start is with a discussion between Julian Baggini and Lawrence Krauss: www.theguardian.com/science/2012/sep/09/science-philosophy-debate-julian-baggini-lawrence-krauss. You could broaden out this discussion by asking students what they think science is and also by exploring the links between philosophy and other subjects, such as history, literature and art.

Where do we fit in?

"What is the place for humanity in the universe described by science?"

Metaphysics is a jigsaw puzzle in which we are one of the pieces and the universe is the rest of the picture.

What is the place for humanity in the universe? Asking this question takes us straight to the heart of many of the central questions of philosophy. The question implies that the way we understand philosophical questions is itself affected by changes in our knowledge of the universe.

Without doubt, science has transformed the way we view reality. Much philosophical debate concerns the implications of this for our understanding of ourselves and our place in the cosmos. One of the biggest metaphysical debates of all is that between naturalism (the theory that the only things that exist are those which science describes) and supernaturalism (which holds there are things which cannot be explained scientifically).

A good way of helping students see the connection between this sort of metaphysics and ordinary life is to start with a series of (real or invented) newspaper headlines and ask them what philosophical issues they raise. For example:

- Scientists discover the events that happened at the beginning of time.
- Will discovery of the 'God' particle bring an end to religion?
- The gene for crime has been identified.
- Scientists identify the part of the brain which creates the experience of love.
- The genes which control the aging process may soon be found.
- Human cloning is now possible.

Bonus idea ★

There are many elements to the controversy over naturalism and it makes an excellent topic for classroom debate. It is worth running the debate both as an interesting exercise in itself and also because it can help to raise issues for further exploration. If you do run the debate, you can use it to stimulate further philosophical reflection about presuppositions. For example, how do we go about forming our metaphysical beliefs? What counts as evidence for or against a metaphysical position?

Identity parade

"Who am I?"

It is human nature to be fascinated by human nature. This fascination is a rich philosophical stimulus.

As well as scientific issues and ethical controversies, questions about personal identity are a rich stimulus to philosophical inquiry. As Pope put it, 'the proper study of mankind is man'. For students discovering the world of philosophy at a time when they are also beginning to question their own identity, it makes sense to explore the links between philosophical ideas and the way in which we each understand ourselves.

I try to bring out this connection wherever possible. Sometimes, as when the existence of souls is the topic of connection, the link is obvious. But you can use connections to the fascinating issue of personal identity to bring otherwise dry topics alive.

The topic of personal identity is a rich one for stimulating students to think about what it means for to be 'the same'. By virtue of what is it true that I am the same person today that I was yesterday (or a year ago, or ten years ago)? Is it strictly true that I am the same? One way of exploring this is to put a range of possibilities in front of students and ask them how they react. For example:

- Are you still the same person if you change your entire wardrobe of clothes?
- Are you still the same person if you lose your memory?
- If you had a face transplant, would you still be the same person?
- If you had a brain transplant, would you still be the same person?

Making use of MOOCs

"There are some terrific open-access courses out there now!"

Thanks to the advent of Massive Open Online Courses, you and your students have access to the world's best philosophers.

The creation in recent years of 'MOOCs' (Massive Open Online Courses) has the potential to revolutionise education in many ways. As well as the obvious advantage of giving your students a chance to listen to some of the world's greatest philosophical thinkers, the sheer variety of courses means that you can present students with a diet which is both rich and varied.

How should material like this be used? Here are some tips:

- Check the level. There is a difference between secondary school students and undergraduates so choose carefully to make sure that the material is appropriate.
- Be selective. Students will usually benefit more from listening to a well-chosen ten to 15 minute extract than an entire lecture.
- Use a variety of sources. Don't just stick to a single source, however good. Use philosophers with opposing views.
- Use the material to teach study skills. Students will happily listen to a video clip – but may need to be prompted to make notes.
- Use the material to stimulate debate. We learn philosophy by doing philosophy. A good lecture is one that stimulates thought, not one that does the thinking for us.
- Teach students to be content curators. Ask students to select good material themselves, then write a short introduction and post it on a discussion forum, for others to access and respond to.

Talking philosophy

Part 3

Where will you sit?

"Changing the layout of the classroom can make a real difference to how you and the students interact."

It is worth thinking about classroom layout and trying different arrangements, depending on the type of activity you want to see happen.

Teaching tip

Think about how relaxed you want to be with students. If you have the option, putting some soft chairs into the classroom, or even an old sofa, can create a great 'break-out' space for tutorial discussions. You probably won't want to use this all the time, but it can provide a welcome change from a more formal classroom arrangement.

What message is being sent to students by the way you have arranged your classroom? According to the traditional pattern, students sit in rows, ready to listen to the teacher dispensing wisdom from the front. There may be a time and place for that, but it is unlikely to be the best arrangement if you want to promote inquiry-based learning, with plenty of discussion and debate. It is worth experimenting with different arrangements of chairs and tables, with a view to getting the best possible match of the physical configuration of the space in the room to the type of activity that is going on. Here are some suggestions:

- Round table arrangements work well for discussion. A circle of chairs, or an arrangement of seats around a central table, creates a more equal, democratic feel. You may feel the need to differentiate yourself from the group a little; you can do this by picking a higher chair or creating a little more space around yourself.
- If you want to mix-and-match teacher-led talk with discussion and debate, a U shaped arrangement of tables around the room will allow for both.
- If you have space in the classroom, you can create different arrangements for different types of activity: a space with rows set up for whiteboard-centred teaching and a 'break-out' area for discussion or small-group tutorials.

Socratic gadfly

"You have to be prepared to challenge the things your students say."

Critical questioning might seem annoying but it is vital in stimulating students to think for themselves.

Socrates became famous for his habit of challenging people to explain the meaning of their ideas. He likened himself to a 'gadfly': it was his job to sting the people of Athens, whom he likened to a lazy horse, with his probing questions until they woke up to the fact that they were living their lives on the basis of unexamined ideas.

Students often come to philosophy thinking that 'any idea is as good as any other'. They will be surprised to find that this is not so: some ideas are better than others. Getting clear about what an idea really means is a crucial part of philosophical inquiry. It is your job to ask the challenging, probing questions, which will stimulate students to begin examining their ideas for themselves, and bring them to realise that there is an important difference between talking sense and nonsense.

While students do need to be challenged, it is important to do this in a gentle, respectful manner.

- Explain to students that in philosophy, all ideas are open to question.
- Be prepared to let students challenge your ideas too.
- Explain that there is a difference between a challenge to the logical coherence of an idea and a personal attack. Argument can be robust and rigorous without degenerating into a personal slanging match.

Teaching tip

When you do critique a student's thoughts, use the gentlest possible language. Use phrases such as 'If I've understood you correctly, what you are saying is...' or 'If what you are saying is this, then I wonder how you'd respond to the objection that...'.

Socratic investigation

"I enjoy lessons when we work our way through a philosophical investigation together."

Some of the best philosophy lessons of all are those in which you and the class investigate a philosophical problem together.

One of the best things about teaching philosophy and ethics is the chance to explore a problem together with students. Some of the most rewarding lessons are those in which you and the class become 'joint-inquirers' in the search for philosophical truth.

For this to work well you need to know roughly which direction the investigation should take, but also be ready to respond to novel suggestions from the class. It is important to have the right questions ready to take the investigation forward.

A good starting question might be: Are colours in the mind or in the world? After some initial discussion, ask students to try to state the conditions under which the sentence 'The tomato is red.' Would be true. Is it true that the tomato is red if it looks red? Students might spot the problem here: it might not look red under some conditions (for example, at night). Also, it might not look red to some observers (for example, dogs).

A next step is to offer a refined definition: 'The tomato is red if it looks red in normal conditions to normal observers.' But what counts as 'normal'? Does this definition support the view that colours are in the world or in the mind? A sequence of appropriately chosen questions will lead the class up to this point, and from here you can open the discussion out to explore students' ideas, as well as further possible implications.

Taking it further

The question of whether qualities exist in the mind or in the world is profoundly important. You might want to point out to students that a similar issue arises with qualities such as beauty, or moral value. For an audio-essay exploring the issue further, listen to the podcast at the hashtag below.

#isgrassgreen

Managing the extremes

"Some students say too much – others say nothing at all!"

In any group, there are some students who are happy to talk a great deal, and others who prefer not to speak at all. Getting a balanced discussion takes some planning.

What happens when you launch your carefully planned inquiry-based lesson with a well-judged question, only to be greeted by silence? Or what if someone has so much to say that no one else can get a word in edgeways? To avoid these problems, you need some strategies up your sleeve. Here are some suggestions:

Teaching tip

A very talkative class member can be asked to chair a discussion. Explain to the student that the job of chair is to give a (brief!) introduction then ask questions that encourage other group members to contribute.

- Plan to have two or three discussion activities per lesson. If one discussion goes flat, move swiftly on to the next one.
- Spend time explaining why group discussion is important. Some students might think that it is a waste of time – why not just listen while the teacher tells them 'what they need to know'? But philosophical inquiry is, by its nature, discursive: we develop our philosophical understanding by putting forward ideas, and responding when other people critique them. Discussion is essential, not an optional add-on.
- Work at building confidence. It isn't easy to speak out for the first time, so make sure you encourage the quieter members of the group and show appreciation for their contribution.
- Vary the format. Ask students to discuss in pairs or small groups then invite one person from each pair to report back.
- Quiet students may be happier describing other people's ideas than offering their own. So after a small group discussion, invite each person to summarise another group member's ideas.

Brain games

"A fun way to work out what I think."

Games which allow students to work out their own philosophical views are a good starting point for discussion.

Teaching tip

Following this initial 'diagnostic' activity, it can be fruitful to discuss the questions one at a time, exploring arguments for and against each answer.

On some topics, students might have clear views of their own. They might recognise themselves as atheists, believers or agnostics, for example. But on other topics, they might not know what they themselves think. What do they think about the basis of ethics? What is their view about the best answer to the mind–body problem? A good activity for helping them to identify their own philosophical position is to use an adaptation of the magazine quizzes used to work out things like personality type.

Ask students to answer a set of multiple-choice questions, the answers to which correspond to different philosophical theories. By seeing their most frequent answers, they can identify their own position on the spectrum of philosophical thought about a topic. Here is an example:

1. Do you think the mind could exist outside the body? (a) Yes (b) No
2. What do you think consciousness is?
   (a) Something happening in the soul
   (b) A brain process
3. Do animals have minds? (a) No, since they don't have souls (b) Yes, if their brain processes are similar to ours
4. Are you made of purely physical stuff?
   (a) Yes (b) No

Taking it further

Students might want to discuss the classification system which this game presupposes. For example, must you be either a dualist or a materialist? Could you be a dualist and also believe that animals have minds? (Descartes didn't – but other dualists would disagree...)

Explain that the answers correspond to two different philosophical theories about the mind–body problem. Mainly (a) means they are probably a mind–body dualist. If they have answered mainly (b) they are a materialist.

From discussion to debate

"You really begin to think about an idea when you are asked to defend it in a debate."

Once students have identified philosophical ideas they agree with, a natural next step is to stage a debate.

There is great value in getting students involved in debate. It is when you try to construct a reasoned defence of a proposition that you really get a feel for its philosophical merits.

One way of doing this is to follow the medieval model and ask students to defend a thesis, regardless of their own beliefs. But you can also set up a debate as a natural follow-on activity from a classroom discussion designed to help students identify their own beliefs (as in Idea 38).

For example, I sometimes start a class discussion by asking that old chestnut of a question: If a tree falls over in a forest, and there is no one around, does it make a sound? Students usually divide in their response to this, and after some discussion I then explain that a major philosophical debate has gone on about just this issue. Realists believe that there is a world that exists independently of our minds. Anti-realists assert that reality is mind-dependent.

Having explained this distinction, students are then asked to vote on whether they are realists or anti-realists. The class is then divided into realist and anti-realist camps. The two sides are asked to develop arguments in favour of their point of view. Depending on the numbers involved, you might choose to have two teams on either side. The stage is then set for a whole-class debate.

Teaching tip

Explain to students that in philosophical arguments, it is possible to criticise someone else's ideas without making a personal attack on them. You can respect a person, but still disagree with what they say. The appropriate way to express criticism is using logic and evidence, not point-scoring or personal remarks.

Preparing to debate

"Successful debates don't just happen – they need careful preparation."

Student debates can work really well provided the students have prepared properly. They need guidance to avoid some of the pitfalls.

Teaching tip

Spend some time in advance helping the students to think through the arguments they will use. You don't want them to get up to speak only to discover they have nothing worth saying!

Class debates can be lively, exciting and rewarding learning experiences; equally, they can become rowdy arguments with little educational benefit. Students need to be given guidance about how debates work, and they need to spend time preparing properly if the debate is to be worthwhile. Here are some pointers:

- Explain to students that debating is a formal process, in which there is a defined proposition (the motion) which is being argued.
- Establish teams of proposers and opposers. Realistically, a team will be two or three strong at most. You could run two or three mini-debates on different motions, to ensure that everyone gets to speak. You might also want to ensure that each team is reasonably balanced in ability terms – you don't want things to be too one-sided!
- Establish ground rules for your debate, including the length of speeches (for example, two or three minutes, or five at the most).
- This is one occasion where PowerPoint can be avoided, in the interest of discouraging students from simply reading out pre-prepared speeches.
- Traditionally, debates begin with speeches proposing the motion then speeches opposing the motion. Finally, time is allowed for rebuttals in which both sides respond to each other's arguments.

- Rebuttal is difficult as it means that students have to be ready to think on their feet. You might prefer a simpler model, in which both teams speak followed by a question and answer session in which the audience can participate.
- Preparation for a debate can take place through a combination of work in lessons and homework. Ask students to carry out research in their own time to find arguments they can use in the debate, then allocate them some time during lessons to allow them to discuss arguments within their team.

Taking it further

For more debating tips, see the Debating Matters website: www. debatingmatters.com/ getinvolved/toptips. If your students really enjoy debating you can also find details on this website in the 'Get involved' section of debating competitions your students could enter.

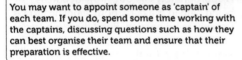

Bonus idea ★

You may want to appoint someone as 'captain' of each team. If you do, spend some time working with the captains, discussing questions such as how they can best organise their team and ensure that their preparation is effective.

Running a formal debate

"Order, order!"

For a debate to work well, it needs to be well-chaired.

As well as careful preparation, successful debates need to be chaired firmly and fairly. Here are some pointers:

- Before the first speech, make sure the room is appropriately laid out. If the debate is being held in the classroom, amplification is unlikely to be needed. But if there is a larger venue, check that microphones are working.
- Prepare space for the teams to be assembled at the front – you don't want time to be wasted in the middle of the debate as speakers make their way to the front.
- Check that the speakers are aware of the ground rules, and explain these to the audience as well.
- Decide whether you will allow 'points of information' to be made. Unless your students are experienced debaters, it is best to restrict any interruptions and simply have questions at the end.
- Take a few minutes to set the scene and introduce the motion, but don't go on too long as time is tight. Invite the propositioner to speak, then start a stop-watch or keep a close eye on the clock.
- One of the chair's main jobs is timekeeping. You might want to prepare time cards (for example, 'One minute remaining') to slip to speakers when needed. You might also need to find a gavel (or whistle!) to bring proceedings to order or call a halt to an over-long speech.

- Debates are exciting and, in the middle of the excitement, people can get carried away with themselves. So be ready to intervene if the speakers, or audience, go off-topic or make unhelpful remarks.
- Decide at the outset whether you will end the debate with a vote (and perhaps have a pre-debate vote as well). Make sure you have a mechanism for gathering votes if the audience is large (for example, Yes and No slips which can be placed in a box).
- Wrap the debate up at the end by thanking the speakers and the audience.
- You may want to give feedback to the speakers, either as a group, or individually. Sometimes it is best to make brief comments at the end of the debate, then give fuller feedback later, when the speakers have had a chance to calm down after the excitement.

Bonus idea ★

Watch the opening speeches in a philosophical debate from the institute of arts and ideas (www.iai. tv) then ask your students to continue the debate for themselves, responding to the points made on the video. You could then play the rest of the video to see if the same points come up. When discussing a debate that you have watched together, invite students to think about the logical structure of the arguments and also to consider how well the participants spoke. Were any particular points especially memorable, and if so, why did they stand out? Thinking in this way can assist students in planning for their own debates.

Running tutorials

"Being asked to read my essay to the rest of the class was scary but I'm glad I did."

Tutorials which begin with students reading their essays aloud can be valuable for both the individual student and the rest of the group.

In tutorial sessions, a student is invited to read out an essay they have written. This forms the basis of discussion, with feedback from the teacher.

The tutorial model has several benefits. The student gets immediate feedback, which can come from the teacher or others in the group. Of course, this can be intimidating, so you may need to explain that the point of reading the essay out is for it to serve as a starting point for discussion – not so that others can focus on its perceived weaknesses.

A tutorial like this can work very well in a small group, but provided the student is sufficiently confident there is no reason why the essay should not be read in front of the whole class.

While the essay is being read, jot down a few points to use as starters for discussion. You don't need to give a detailed critique – it is more a matter of picking up on general ideas or issues which the essay raises.

One problem with basing lessons around what a student's work is that the essay may turn out to be a poor discussion starter – either because it is so poor, or, less commonly, because it is so good that no one feels they have anything to add. It is a good idea to read the essays in advance, and select one that seems to be at a helpful and realistic level.

Student-led seminars

"Just occasionally, it is worth handing over the reins."

Letting students take charge of a seminar helps them to develop a sense of responsibility for learning and gives you a valuable opportunity to observe the group from another perspective.

This idea depends on having one or two confident, mature students in your group who you feel you can trust to take a lead. It is similar to the idea of a student tutorial (Idea 42), except that in this case, as well as a student presenting a paper as a discussion starter, another student takes on the role of chairing the discussion.

As well as needing students with the confidence and maturity to do this effectively, you need to make sure that the stimulus material is appropriate. For seminars like this, I normally browse the web to find a short, stimulating, controversial article which raises some interesting philosophical points. A good example would be a newspaper feature exploring a topic from ethics or philosophy of religion. Ideally, everyone in the group should read the article beforehand.

The student who is chairing the seminar then invites the introducer to give a short overview of the article, and perhaps adds some thoughts of their own, before opening the discussion to the rest of the group.

You may need to have a short chat with the student chairperson, to make sure that they have a few questions up their sleeve to help keep the conversation going. Remind them too that it is good if everyone says something, so they should look for opportunities to bring quiet members of the group into the discussion.

Teaching tip

If all goes well, you shouldn't need to say anything. As well as the benefits that come from giving students real responsibility for the learning process, student-led seminars give you a chance to observe the interactions among the group and gain a deeper appreciation of the level of understanding and philosophical skills of the participating students.

Oral presentation skills

"The golden rule of oral presentations is: less is more!"

There are lots of opportunities for oral presentation during philosophy and ethics lessons, so it makes sense to teach students how to speak well.

Teaching tip

Practice makes perfect. If students are doing class presentations, encourage them to rehearse in front of friends or even on their own.

As so much philosophical learning happens through discussion and debate, it makes sense to spend some time teaching students some basic oral presentation skills. Here are some suggestions.

- Begin by making the point about the difference between what people hear and what is said by having a quick game of Chinese whispers.
- When it comes to oral presentation, less is most definitely more! Ask students for examples of effective speeches they have heard (these could be in films, in lessons, assemblies ...). In almost all cases, there is a clear, simple take-home message.
- Another good rule is: Say what you are going to say, then say it, then say that you've said it. It does no harm to say the same thing in different ways. If you make the same point three times over (as I've now done), it is more likely to be remembered. A well-structured talk will contain an introduction that sets the scene and establishes rapport with the audience, a main section, and a conclusion, which reminds listeners of the main point of the talk.
- Avoid death by PowerPoint. Warn students not to make the mistake of putting lots of text on a PowerPoint, then turning towards the screen and reading it out.

Taking it further

Aristotle taught that the elements of rhetoric (effective public speech) were logos (logical reasoning), ethos (personal style) and pathos (appeal to emotion). Listen to some effective presentations (for example, from TED talks, an organisation which invites inspirational speakers and world leaders to give short talks) and analyse the way speakers incorporate these elements.

Keep the conversation going

"Dialogue is a great way to explore all sides of a philosophical issue."

Many of the greatest philosophical writings take the form of dialogues. Why not ask students to write their own?

Philosophy is by its nature a dialogical subject: it consists in an unending conversation about the nature of reality and the ideas by which we live. From Plato's dialogues to the dialogues of Hume, Schopenhauer or Berkeley, much of the best philosophical writing has been cast in the form of dialogue.

Asking students to write in this form is a great way of encouraging them to think about all sides of an argument.

One option here is to read an extract from one of the great dialogues and then stop and ask students to carry the dialogue on themselves. This sort of exercise works best as a synoptic activity at the end of a unit, by which time students should have some ideas of the arguments that figure in a debate.

For this to work well, you will need to spend time analysing the text, to ensure that students understand the positions of the characters and the logic of the arguments. In some dialogues, specific philosophers are represented (for example, in Berkeley's dialogues between Hylas and Philonous, Hylas represents Locke and Philonous represents Berkeley). You could read the extract in class with different students taking on the role of the different characters.

Teaching tip

Hume's wonderful 'Dialogues concerning natural religion' can be found here: www. davidhume.org. Berkeley's dialogues are here: www. earlymoderntexts.com/ pdfs/berkeley1713.pdf.

Taking it further

Read some extracts from the 'objections and replies' other philosophers wrote to Descartes, then ask students to write a letter of objection to Descartes. See www. earlymoderntexts.com/ pdfs/descartes1642_2.pdf.

Reading and researching

Part 4

Philosophical scaffolding

"Put up the scaffolding then hand the tools to the students to see what they can build."

If you want students to learn to research independently, you need to give them a structure to build around.

There is a long-running debate between those who think we should teach 'skills' and those who think we need to teach 'knowledge'. Is there a way to combine both approaches?

One idea is to look at the material on a particular topic, and separate it into two parts: the 'scaffolding', or structural elements, and the rest of the content. If you provide students with the necessary structural framework for them to begin making sense of a topic, they will then be in a position to engage in meaningful research, and fill in the gaps for themselves. Here are a few examples:

- When teaching the philosophy of mind, introduce students to dualism and materialism (see Idea 38). Then ask them to do some web research to identify three arguments for each theory.
- When discussing the topic of the nature of personal identity, you could distinguish between the 'essentialist' theory that there is an inner essence to a person, and the constructivist view that the self is something we construct. Ask students to research the topic of women's rights, using this distinction to categorise different arguments.
- Explore the difference between naturalism and supernaturalism, and ask students to identify the presence of these different frameworks in the debate about the rationality of belief in miracles.

Taking it further

The idea of philosophical frameworks is a useful one for helping students to get some feel for the way ideas within a topic area are organised. However, labelling positions can sometimes lead to distortion, since the complex ideas of philosophers can rarely be reduced to simple definable 'isms', such as materialism, realism and so forth. The issue of whether using 'isms' is a helpful simplification or a misleading distortion is worth discussing with your class.

Argument identification

"Before you can evaluate an argument, you need to work out what the argument actually is."

It helps if you provide a framework to assist students when identifying arguments.

Philosophy is all about argument. We want students to learn how to think critically about arguments they read, and create their own arguments as well. Before they can do this, however, they need to have some feel for the structure of argument.

The skill of argument identification is one that needs to be taught. A great deal of time could be spent exploring formal logic, but if your main aim is to equip students to think critically about the merits of philosophical and ethical ideas you will need something that can be applied simply and quickly.

Suggest the following framework:

- In any given piece of text, ask students to identify the conclusion of the argument – the point which the author is trying to prove. Linguistic indicators can be helpful here (for example, 'therefore ...', 'it follows that .... ', 'we can conclude that ...').
- Once the conclusion has been identified, ask students to describe the reasons that are given in support of this conclusion. It is worth pointing out that people often mix several arguments together. You might want to separate them out with separate argument maps on a board.
- Often, but not always, people state and then try to respond to counter-arguments against their conclusions. It is worth asking students to identify any counter-arguments and responses in the text.

Teaching tip

To sum up: the elements students are looking for when reading arguments are:

- conclusion
- argument
- counter-argument
- response to counter-argument.

The five Ws

"Research begins with asking questions."

The concept of the five Ws — who, what, where, why and when? — is a useful tool for students to use when beginning research.

On many philosophical and ethical topics, we will want our students to be able to carry out their own research. Where do you start? Research begins when we ask questions of the sources we are using. A good tool for getting students started is the 'five Ws': who, what, where, why and when? These questions are deliberately open-ended, and in most documents, you can find answers to most of them.

You can try the five Ws on more or less any documentary source. Newspaper articles work well. Select an article on an interesting topic (it could be a report of a concert or a sporting event). Ask students to read through it and find answers to each of the five W questions.

They will probably spot that the questions can be asked in more than one way. For example, the question 'Where?' could mean: 'Where did the event happen?' or 'Where was it reported?'. 'Why?' is also rich in possibilities; explanation can take many different forms.

When you have discussed the source using the five Ws, explain to students that the process of research begins with asking questions. The five W questions may not always be the best ones to ask, but they are often a good place to start. What matters most of all is that, whatever they read, they read critically, asking questions about the source rather than just taking it for granted.

Easy citations and bibliographies

"Creating references has never been easier."

There are a number of free computer tools to simplify the process of creating references.

Suppose that you have asked your students to carry out a research project on a philosophical or ethical topic. One thing that you might want them to do is to create proper citations and a bibliography. It is worth explaining to students why this is considered an important part of academic writing. Your argument is stronger if it can be linked clearly to credible sources and there is also the important moral point of making clear the difference between your own ideas and those you have derived from others.

One important point to emphasise to students is that they need to keep track of research sources as they go – it can be very difficult to 'back-track' at the end if they haven't built their bibliography during the research process.

Thankfully, creating references and a bibliography is now extremely easy. Here is how it can be done if you are using Microsoft Word Windows.

- Click on the 'References' toolbar.
- Click on the 'Insert Citation' button.
- Click on 'Add New Source'.

You can then input the source details. The computer creates an 'in-text citation' for you. Better still, at the end of your report, click on 'References' then 'Bibliography' and the bibliography will appear! These functions speed up the process of creating citations and bibliographies enormously.

Teaching tip

For guidance on the creation of references, type 'guidance on referencing' into a search engine. Universities publish extensive guidance about how to reference appropriately.

Taking it further

The same functions are available to Mac users – you need to start with the 'Toolbox' then click on the 'Citations' button.

If you want to use other programs, have a look at 'reference management software' on Wikipedia for suggestions.

The golden key

"Research is so much easier when you find a good source to start from."

When students are researching, sometimes a single source can unlock the door and lead them straight to the heart of the topic.

Teaching tip

Helping your students to find a 'golden key' article is an example of effective research facilitation. Independent research is a challenge for students who lack the knowledge of a subject that enables them to discriminate between crucially important sources and ones that are peripheral. By helping them to start in the right place, you can prevent some of the frustration that can occur when students spend a long time looking for materials but find little of real value.

I once had to write six 5000 word research essays in the space of 12 weeks. A trick which I learnt, which I now teach to students when I'm setting them project work, is to look for the 'golden key'. This is a single article which provides you with an overview of the topic you are writing about. If you find a golden key article, you can use it to open the door on a research field.

The point to emphasise to students is that if they do find a 'golden key' article, they should use it ruthlessly. By following up the authors mentioned in the article, or cited in the bibliography, you can quickly find a lot of really useful source material and save yourself a great deal of time spent going down blind alleys. The golden key can open the door and put you on a pathway that takes you straight to the heart of the topic.

Here are some rich starting points:

The Stanford Encyclopedia of Philosophy: plato.stanford.edu.

The Internet Encyclopedia of Philosophy: www.iep.utm.edu.

Philosophy Bites: www.philosophybites.com

Bioethics Bites: www.philosophybites.com/bio-ethics.

OpenDOAR: www.opendoar.org (OpenDOAR is an excellent starting point for searching open-access repositories).

The two-stage research rocket

"Planning research is much easier if you understand the stages in the process."

The first stage in research is gathering source materials. The second stage is asking what the sources mean.

You've asked your students to research a philosophical topic. Most students will understand this to mean going on the internet to find material which is relevant to the question they have been asked. This is a very basic understanding of research. I explain to students that research is a two-stage process. First comes the 'finding out' stage, in which they collect source material. But after this, there is an important stage when they have a look at the materials they have found, and ask what they mean. This second stage – the analytical stage – is what lifts research beyond simple acquisition of information, turning it into a process which can lead to genuine understanding.

In the first stage, students will be:
- Web-browsing
- Reading books (hopefully)
- Visiting the library (perhaps!)
- Interviewing people.

During the second stage, students will be:
- Compiling the information
- Making use of the five Ws (see Idea 48)
- Re-writing it in their own words
- Thinking about how it all fits together
- Asking what it means in relation to the question they have been asked.

Students need to understand that they can't do the second stage until the first is complete; equally, if they spend all their time just acquiring information, the level of their research will never be more than basic.

Teaching tip

When you set a research task, you might want to explain which tasks you expect to see happening at the start, and at what point in time they should move from the first to the second stage.

Taking it further

Explain to students that research is a process of finding things out and that effective research involves in-depth investigation. Ask them to write a list of sources that they plan to use. Then look at the list with them and discuss whether they have just gone for the most easily accessible sources, or whether they have also included some which will be more challenging to find.

Vox pop

"It is always interesting to find out what people think about philosophical and ethical questions."

Carrying out your own survey, or using data from published surveys, can illuminate the discussion of a philosophical topic.

Carrying out a survey of public opinion, or doing research to find out what other surveys have to say, can help to suggest new ideas and give a sense of which opinions tend to be most popular. It also provides an opportunity to gain an insight into why people think as they do – and this can in turn lead into deeper, richer philosophical engagement.

One of the swiftest, easiest ways of creating a simple survey is via the website surveymonkey (www.surveymonkey.com). I usually give students a few pointers, such as:

- Don't ask too many questions. People don't have much time, so limit it to five to seven questions at most.
- Closed questions are better than open, since you can do something with the data (for example, construct bar charts or do some simple statistics).
- You might want to include one open question at the end of the survey, so people have the option of replying in more detail.
- Questions should be neutral, not biased.
- Once created, the survey can be sent out using a link in an email message.
- Typically, students might survey ten to 20 of their friends or family.

Question time

"Do you mind if I ask you a few questions about your philosophical beliefs?"

Asking students to interview other people about their philosophical beliefs can be an effective way of starting a discussion.

An activity in which students are asked to interview someone else to find out about their philosophical beliefs can work well for a number of reasons. Firstly, preparing for an interview involves thinking about the best questions to ask to find out what someone really thinks. Secondly, the interview itself is a form of philosophical dialogue, albeit one in which the interviewer may know in advance what they are going to ask. Finally, a class session in which students report back on the interview they carried out can serve as a good starter for further discussion and investigation of the philosophical issues raised during the interview. I find that students may be happier to report what other people think than to venture their own opinion, so this activity can be good for a whole-class discussion in which everyone is expected to say something. Bear in mind that if the comments of the interviewee are going to be shared with the group, the interviewee should be told this, as they may prefer to remain anonymous.

The interview can serve to reinforce the 'argument – counter-argument – response' model described in Idea 47. In briefing students before they carry out their interview, you might suggest that they ask questions designed to elicit information about the interviewee's beliefs, the reasons they give for these beliefs, and the way in which they respond to possible counter-arguments.

Teaching tip

I have seen this technique work well in the context of topics in the philosophy of religion, such as beliefs about the origins of the universe. Sensitively handled, it could also be used for exploration of ethical issues such as abortion or euthanasia.

Taking it further

If technical issues such as stem cell research are to be explored, I sometimes suggest to students that they produce a fact sheet with a summary of the issue to give to the interviewee beforehand.

Philosophical argument

Part 5

What does it mean?

"An investigation of the meaning of a word is a good way into philosophical discussion."

Wittgenstein stated that to find the meaning of a word we need to investigate its use in language. Linguistic analysis is an important philosophical technique.

A simple activity for introducing students to the important philosophical topic of linguistic meaning is to ask them what they think the meaning of a word like 'table' is.

A natural answer is that the meaning of such a word is the thing that it stands for (i.e. 'table' means table). However, it doesn't take much thought to see the limitations of this theory.

At this point you could introduce Wittgenstein's more flexible account of meaning, according to which the meaning of a word is the way it is used. To explain the meaning of the word 'table', we have to think about the sentences in which the word is used. But we also need to think about the role the word plays in life: Why do we need the word? What functions does talking about tables play in life?

Wittgenstein's theory helpfully links language use to the rest of human life. Asking students to build up an account of the meaning a word plays in their life is a helpful way of showing how language use connects to life, and also of highlighting that giving meaning to a word is a more complicated activity than simply naming an object.

Taking it further

Take a word which philosophers discuss, such as truth, knowledge, beauty, the mind, God, the soul, free will, goodness, identity, time or space, and ask students to carry out a Wittgensteinian investigation into the ways the word is used. Note that there will almost certainly be multiple uses of the word. Remind them to explore the connections between the word and the role it plays in life.

Concept mapping

"Don't fall into the trap of thinking that every word has a single meaning."

Many words have multiple meanings. It is helpful to try to map some of the different ways a word is used.

As even a quick look at a dictionary shows, many words have multiple meanings – a fact often forgotten when people ask for 'the' definition of a word like knowledge or truth. A good way of exploring the different meanings of a word is to work on a concept mapping exercise with students.

Suppose we wanted to do a concept map of the word 'mind'. A first step would be to identify different uses of the word. Ask the class to generate a list of sentences in which the word is used. For example:

- 'What's on your mind?'
- 'I can't make up my mind.'
- 'It completely slipped my mind.'

Next, ask students to paraphrase each sentence without the use of the word 'mind'. For example, the above three sentences are roughly equivalent to these three:

- 'What are you thinking about?'
- 'I can't decide what to do.'
- 'I forgot about it.'

Finally, explore what these paraphrases show us about what we mean when we speak of the mind. There are links to thinking, decision making and memory here – what other links can students think of? Are any of these usages more important than others?

Taking it further

For a short philosophical investigation of this topic search for #whatisthemind on Twitter. You will find a YouTube video there to watch with your class. Afterwards ask them to discuss 'what is the mind'.

#whatisthemind

Compare and contrast

"Let's put this idea side-by-side with another."

We can get a better understanding of a concept when we compare it with another, looking at similarities and differences.

Some concepts are vague: there is no precise definition of the number of grains of sand in a heap. But even if there aren't precise boundaries to a concept, we can still help to make it clearer by comparing and contrasting it with other, related but distinct, concepts.

For example, suppose you are thinking about the nature of science. One way to get students thinking about this is to ask them to compare and contrast science and religion, science and art, or science and history.

Questions to discuss with the class include:

- In what ways are these things similar?
- In what ways are they different?
- Can one of the terms in the pair be used to explain the other?
- Is one thing more important than the other?

Students tend to compartmentalise their ideas about concepts like these: science is a subject they study in science lessons; art, history and religion are studied in other lessons. The idea that there might be interesting points of similarity and differences to be explored will probably not have occurred to them. But by putting these ideas side-by-side, they can begin to get a clearer sense of their 'shape', and think for themselves about the extent to which they overlap.

Taking it further

Ask students how they would represent their ideas about a pair of concepts on a diagram. This could be a mind-map, or it could be a Venn diagram. For example, if they drew circles to represent science and religion, would they overlap or be separate? Would one be inside the other?

Sharpening up definitions

"That's a good starting point but we're not there yet."

Work together on refining a definition as a good example of how to work through a philosophical problem.

A good way of exemplifying some of the techniques of philosophical analysis is to work with a class on a rough definition of a concept to see what needs to be done to turn it into a better one. One example of this is thinking through the concept of knowledge.

I usually begin by asking students to define knowledge. This raises the problem that there are different forms – there is knowledge that things are true (propositional knowledge), knowing how to do things, knowledge of persons (I know my family), and probably more besides. So we then narrow our focus to propositional knowledge. Ask students the difference between knowledge and belief. What do we have to add to believing that there are birds in the garden, to turn it into knowledge? Usually, with a little prompting, everyone can come to agree that while belief can be true or false, knowledge must be true. If someone thinks they know that squares have five sides, they have just made a mistake.

So now we have a definition of knowledge as 'true belief'. Is that all there is to it? What if I truly guessed that there are 18 birds in my garden at the moment? That wouldn't count as knowledge. Students can usually see that we have to add another condition, relating to justification – I need to be able to back up my claim to knowledge. If I have counted, and so formed a true belief, it looks like I know.

So we reach the classical ('tripartite') definition of propositional knowledge as 'true justified belief'.

Teaching tip

Students may not accept that knowledge has to be true. This is often because they confuse real knowledge with what is believed to be knowledge. Point out that although some people thought they knew that the earth is flat, they couldn't really have known this, as it isn't true that the earth is flat.

Taking it further

Once you have established the tripartite definition, you might like to challenge your students to see if there is more to the story. Mention the Gettier counter-examples and set them the task of researching to find out what else needs to be added to the definition.

Word triples

"See what you can do with these words."

Exploring the differences in meaning among a word triple can help to develop skills in conceptual analysis.

Once students have begun to get a feel for the importance of exploring the meaning of words by using contrasts, a good follow-up activity is to give them a set of three words and ask them to write a short essay explaining the similarities and differences in meaning between them. Word triples for this exercise include:

- Faith, belief, trust
- Belief, truth, knowledge
- Feeling, emotion, sensation
- Picture, image, painting
- Mind, soul, person
- Reasonable, rational, logical.

A good way into this exercise is to ask students to work in groups and brainstorm possible similarities and differences. If they are struggling to find any, ask them to follow the method used in Idea 55:

- Generate a few sentences using each of the words.
- Try to write a paraphrase for each sentence, in which the word is not used.
- When they wrote the paraphrase, did they find they had used one of the other words from the triple?

For example, take the sentence, 'He is a happy soul.'

A paraphrase of this would be: 'He is a happy sort of person'. This points to a link between the concept of the soul and that of a person. Roughly speaking, to talk about the soul is to talk about the sort of person someone is.

Can you move the universe?

"What a weird idea!"

Questioning whether the universe could move can lead students to appreciate how the meaning of a word depends on context.

Wittgenstein proposed that we should think of words as being like tools. One point of this helpful analogy is to remind us that whether a word functions as it should depends on the context in which it is used. A good way to explore the importance of context is to ask the question: Could the whole universe be moved three feet to the left?

The question might need some explanation. It relies on the intuitive distinction between the universe on the one hand (i.e. the planets, stars, galaxies and other material objects in space) and the space within which the material universe exists on the other. If we think that the universe is located within space, it seems to make sense to say that it could be moved to another position. But given that there would be no detectable change as a result of this shift, does it really make sense to say that such a change could occur?

Students may well have different views about this. After some discussion, take a step back from the debate and point out that the question is asking us to think about the meaning of talk about space. Should we think of space as being a great big container, within which the universe is located? Or is space itself part of the universe? Is space more like a set of relationships between objects?

Taking it further

Behind the debate about the location of the universe is the debate about truth and verification: Can there be truths which we can never know? This issue could be explored by asking students to think about whether there are truths about the distant past, which can now no longer be known, and whether there are truths about other people's minds which we can never know for sure (for example – the way red looks to other people).

The language of argument

"Arguments can be good or bad in different ways."

When students are learning to evaluate arguments, it helps to teach them some terminology to use when distinguishing between good and bad arguments.

Teaching tip

To help students grasp this distinction, present a series of arguments and ask them to assess if they are valid. For example, this argument is valid: All ducks are noisy. Oscar is a duck. Therefore Oscar is noisy.

This argument is not valid: To get a car to start, it needs to have petrol in it. Fred's car has petrol in it. Therefore Fred's car will start.

Perhaps Fred's car has a flat battery.

When students are evaluating arguments, they often struggle to find appropriate words to use. They may also not be aware that there are different ways in which arguments can fail. A useful distinction to draw is that between validity and soundness.

An argument is said to be valid if the conclusion follows from the premises. That is, it is not possible for the premises to be true and the conclusion false. An argument is invalid if it is possible for the premises to be true and the conclusion false.

However, an argument may be valid but not have a true conclusion. The conclusion will only be true if the premises are true. The term we use for a valid argument with true premises is 'sound'. What this shows is that when evaluating arguments, two questions should be asked:

- Does the conclusion follow from the premises (is the argument valid)?
- Are the premises true?

It is only when the answer to both of these questions is 'yes' that we have a sound argument.

Looking for the black swan

"It only takes one black swan to refute the statement that all swans are white."

The technique of looking for counter-examples to an argument is a way of testing its validity.

How do we test if an argument is valid? An argument is invalid if the premises could be true, but the conclusion false. A situation in which this happens is called a 'counter-example'. A good way of encouraging students to evaluate arguments critically is to ask them to imagine a counter-example to the argument. This is associated with the discovery of black swans – a counter-example to the argument that if a bird is a swan, it must be white.

For example, you could give students this argument and ask them if they can construct a counter-example: The universe is vast. Therefore there must be life on other planets.

A counter-example to this would be a universe in which life exists only on Earth.

This example is clear-cut and may not provoke much discussion. More interesting cases to argue about include the following.

- Is the existence of God a counter-example to the claim that consciousness depends on the existence of a physical structure such as a brain?
- Is the existence of altruistic behaviour in the animal kingdom (as when a mother bird sacrifices herself for her offspring) a counter-example to the claim that selfishness is natural?
- Is the existence of suffering in the natural world a counter-example to the claim that a perfect God exists?

Teaching tip

While exploring the idea of counter-examples with a group, it is worth pointing out that while finding a counter-example does show that there is a problem with an argument, the fact that you haven't (yet) found a counter-example does not show the argument to be valid. Perhaps the counter-example has yet to be found – which is why it is always wise to be cautious about the conclusions reached using logical inference.

Taking it further

The importance of considering 'black swans' has been explored by Nassim Nicholas Taleb. See his clip at the hashtag below. The issue for discussion is: Do we tend to ignore the possibility of evidence against our favourite theories?

#blackswanproblem

The hitchhiker's guide to the fallacy

"Here's an interesting argument – can you spot any problems with it?"

Make a collection of interesting fallacies. These are great starting points for thinking about good and bad ways of constructing philosophical arguments.

Teaching tip

Keep your own file of these arguments – a 'hitchhiker's guide to the fallacy'. Comments on blogs are a potentially rich source, and there is a website 'www.butterfliesandwheels.org' which has detailed examples of fallacies, with commentary (see the hashtag below).

Fallacies are interesting, both for what they can teach about good and bad ways of constructing arguments, and also because they can show us something interesting about the author whose reasoning has gone awry. The philosopher Susan Stebbing remarked that a particularly good source of fallacies is the letters page in a newspaper. When people are sufficiently worked up about something to write a letter about it, there is a risk that emotion will get the better of logic.

The classification of fallacies is so important in philosophy that many of the most common have names: 'affirming the consequent', 'ad baculum'. These labels can be useful in helping students identify the fallacy formally – but the most important thing is to discuss what has gone wrong with the argument. These arguments are very useful when teaching thinking skills. Discussion of fallacies is a good way of preparing for thinking skills aptitude tests.

Questions to use include:
- Is it sound?
- Is this argument valid?
- Can you think of a counter-example which shows that the conclusion doesn't follow from the premises?
- Can you think of another argument of the same form which clearly doesn't work?
- Why do you think the person who produced this argument committed a fallacy?

Taking it further

Look at some of the fallacies using the hashtag below. Discuss them with students then ask them to do some research to find examples of their own.

#fallacyfile

Argument mapping

"What moves could we make at this point in the argument?"

Providing students with a map of the steps from one position to another can help them make sense of a topic.

Sometimes when students are working through detailed criticism of philosophical theories, they can lose track of the 'big picture'. It can help, therefore, to provide them with an argument map showing how one theory relates to another. For example, in the philosophy of mind, most discussion begins with mind–body dualism. Scientific and philosophical criticism of this theory led to the development of behaviourism. This was in its own turn criticised by materialists. At this point, various threads open up. There are different varieties of materialism (reductive, non-reductive and eliminative) as well as revised versions of dualism (for example, property dualism) and other positions besides (for example, functionalism). As you talk this through you could make an overview map them as follows:

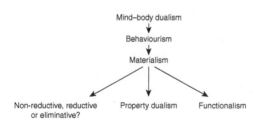

The point of this map is not to imply that students need to choose one of the most recent positions but to show them that there is a generally-accepted trajectory through the discussion of a topic which they should bear in mind when arguing for a particular position.

Argument construction

"Now try to build some arguments of your own."

Students don't find it easy to construct their own arguments. Asking the right questions can help ease them into the process.

The step from analysing other people's arguments to constructing arguments of your own is a difficult one. It is one thing to discuss the faults in an argument you have read from a blog – it is another thing to write your own argument and risk having its faults being pointed out. But it is through this process that students learn to argue better.

There are various steps in the process of constructing your own arguments:

- Identify what you think.
- Write down the reasons for your belief.
- Expand these reasons into arguments in which any hidden premises are clearly stated.
- Compare these arguments with arguments from the philosophical literature to see where more development and defence is needed.
- Test out the arguments in discussion and debate.
- If the argument has faults, see what can be done to fix it (or abandon it and start again!).

When teaching argument construction, don't start with complex arguments (for example, the ontological argument) where students are unlikely to have views of their own. A good context to begin with would be an ethical topic such as lying. So, for example, you could set students the following task:

- Think of as many reasons as you can for why lying is considered wrong.
- Write a list of reasons.

- Look at each reason and see if it relies on hidden assumptions. For example, if the argument is that lying involves manipulating people, a hidden assumption is that it is wrong to manipulate people.
- Search online for philosophical arguments about lying and compare these arguments with ones you have created. A good place to start is www.samharris.org/blog/item/the-high-cost-of-tiny-lies.
- In a small group, discuss your arguments and see if people in the group can think of any weaknesses or spot any fallacious moves.

Taking it further

One way of helping students to develop their argument construction skills is to encourage them to keep a journal in which they make notes on interesting arguments and possible counter-arguments

Bonus idea

A good way of learning about argument construction is to take a bad argument and see if anything can be done to improve it. Julian Baggini has produced a set of 'bad moves' at this website: www.butterfliesandwheels.org/archived/badmoves/. Ask students to select one, discuss what is wrong with it, then try to produce an improved version.

Philosophical Lego

"In philosophy, arguments are the blocks with which you build."

Identifying arguments makes it easier for students to use them as the building blocks from which to construct their philosophical essays.

Philosophy is all about argument. Entire books are written about just one argument. Famous arguments become known by identifying descriptions: the brain-in-a-vat argument, the Chinese Room argument, the cosmological argument and so on.

It is worth pointing this out to students and spending time explaining to them that arguments are like the building blocks out of which philosophical writing is constructed. Philosophers do not write in a vacuum. They write in response to what other philosophers have written and the main focus of most philosophical discussion is on argument. Do particular arguments work? Do they achieve what they claim to? Can they be improved by being re-formulated differently? How does one argument relate to another?

By explicitly teaching students to think in terms of arguments as the building blocks of their essays, you can help them avoid the danger of rambling and failing to get to the point of a question. Suppose for example you ask your students to write an essay on the possibility of artificial intelligence. Instead of letting them simply write their own thoughts, it is worth pointing out that there are some standard arguments about this topic. For example, Searle's Chinese Room argument and the arguments of philosophers who have criticised it are central to the debate.

Taking it further

When students have identified a list of specific arguments that they plan to cover in one of their essays, remind them that they should also consider the way the blocks are joined together. It is best if, having set up an argument, they go on to evaluate it. Essays which are built up of linked sections of argument followed by evaluation are stronger than those with disconnected argumentative sections.

So instead of simply writing out freestyle, and probably missing much that is important in the philosophical discussion, students can be encouraged to construct their essay using arguments as building blocks. An essay plan for the question 'Is artificial intelligence possible?' may begin as follows:

- Paragraph 1: Define terms in the question.
- Paragraph 2: Searle's Chinese Room argument.
- Paragraph 3: The 'systems' objection to the Chinese Room argument.
- Paragraph 4: The 'virtual mind' objection.
- Paragraph 5: Searle's responses to these arguments.

This approach may seem formulaic and restrictive but there is nothing to stop students writing with originality and creativity within such a structure. The main point is that their essay writing will improve once they appreciate that the important thing is to focus their writing on the presentation and discussion of specific arguments.

> **Bonus idea** ★
>
> Give students an article or section from a philosophical book, and ask them to identify and list the building blocks – the specific arguments which it contains. Can they think of catchy titles for these arguments, as a way of helping to make them more memorable?

Frame it

"We don't all think in the same way – and this is what makes philosophy and ethics so interesting."

Teaching frameworks for ethical and philosophical discussion helps students respond to the complexity of the issues.

In philosophy and ethics, we don't all agree about the way to solve problems. It is not just that we don't agree about the right answers – we don't agree about the right frameworks to use when tackling questions. On the face of it, this can be a problem for teachers and students – especially when students want to know 'the right answers', meaning the answers that will get them marks in the exam. But it is possible to turn the inherently open-ended nature of philosophical discussion into an opportunity.

Ask students the question, 'Why is lying generally thought to be wrong?' Answers will probably include:
- People are upset to find they have been deceived.
- Lying is forbidden by the Ten Commandments.
- It's just what we ought to do. We have a duty to tell the truth (and people have a right to know the truth).
- A liar is a dishonest person.

These answers fit into four commonly used ethical frameworks, namely:
- Utilitarianism – the right action is the one which produces the greatest net happiness.
- Divine command theory – the right action is the one commanded by God.
- Rights and duties – the right action is the one which we have a duty to perform.
- Virtue theory – the right action is the one that a virtuous agent would perform.

Making frameworks work

"Let's apply some different frameworks to this problem and see what emerges."

Philosophical and ethical frameworks can be used to help give structure to discussion and to suggest new ideas.

Once students have been taught some ethical or philosophical frameworks, these can be used to enrich discussion and to help students structure their own thinking. For example, having taught the four ethical frameworks mentioned in Idea 66, you can bring these into discussion of further ethical issues, asking questions such as:

- What would a utilitarian say about the ethics of organ donation?
- Is there a divine command perspective that is relevant to the debate about abortion?
- How does the idea of rights and duties apply to the free speech issue?
- Does virtue theory illuminate discussion of the ethics of euthanasia?

These questions serve as a reminder to students of the plurality of approaches that need to be considered. They also show that discussion of specific ethical questions will often lead to discussion of the adequacy of the frameworks which people naturally employ. For example, discussion of the above questions might naturally lead onto discussion of these issues:

- Is the action that creates the greatest happiness necessarily right?
- What makes it right to follow divine commands?
- What is the right to free speech based upon?
- Do some virtues matter more than others?

Teaching tip

Watch out that students don't fall into the trap of thinking that all they have to do is to list what the different theories have to say about a question. The point of the frameworks is to stimulate engagement with the question from a range of perspectives, not to reduce the discussion down to a simple description of different possible answers.

Taking it further

When students are struggling to develop arguments in their essays, remind them of the frameworks. For example, if they are struggling to plan an essay on the ethics of warfare, suggest that they consider what a proponent of each of the four ethical frameworks would say.

The method of disputation

"How would you argue against yourself?"

The method of disputing their own beliefs can help students to strengthen their understanding of them as well as their ability to argue effectively.

In the medieval era, students of theology were trained in 'disputation': assigned a proposition then asked to defend it in debate, regardless of whether they themselves believed it.

Why might it be a good idea to train a novice monk to argue that there is no God? By arguing against yourself, you begin to appreciate the problems within your belief system – the points where you lack good grounds, or where the argument isn't clear. It is also an effective way of preparing for debates, which will involve engaging with and responding to counter-arguments.

In the classroom, you can use this technique in discussion. A good question to ask is: What do you think is the strongest argument against what you have just said?

We are naturally more impressed by arguments which support our beliefs than by those which contradict them, so asking this question is a valuable way of protecting our reasoning processes against bias.

It is important to explain that the point is not to imply that anything can be defended in philosophy, and no position is any better than any other. The method is an exercise in imagination. You are asking students to pretend that they don't believe something they do, as a way of coming to a better understanding of what they believe and the grounds their beliefs rest on, and of strengthening their capacity for effective debate.

Argument formalisation

"Let's lay this argument out formally so we can see what is really going on."

Formalising arguments is often a helpful first step in the process of working out what an argument is actually saying and evaluating its strength.

Sometimes, it helps to lay out an argument formally – as a series of numbered statements, beginning with premises and ending with the main conclusion. Formalisation of argument can be a highly technical process, and sometimes spending time on this can distract from the main issue, which is to get to the point of being able to evaluate the strength of the argument. But on other occasions, it can be really helpful to have a clear, simple version of an argument on the table, with the premises clearly identified.

As an example of an argument that formalises well, consider the 'Kalam cosmological argument', defended by William Lane Craig:

1. The universe began to exist.
2. Whatever begins to exist has a cause.
3. Therefore, the universe has a cause.

You can either begin with this, or begin with a version of the argument in which the structure isn't yet clear and ask students to identify the premises and the conclusion. Once you have a formalised argument on the board, you can swiftly move into evaluation, asking questions such as:

- What is the evidence for the premises?
- If the premises are true, does the conclusion follow? (Is the argument valid?)
- If the conclusion is true, what does this imply? Does this argument prove God exists?

Teaching tip

Teach this technique by demonstration, and then, occasionally, ask students to formalise arguments themselves, in situations where this is likely to prove helpful for further discussion.

Taking it further

Encourage students to use argument formalisation in their essays. It is not always helpful, but often, when there are well-known arguments, having a short, snappy, formalised version of the argument can help to focus the discussion on what is really going on. Being asked to formalise an argument may also show the student that they haven't yet understood what the argument is.

But what do I really think?

"I'm so confused – I don't know what I think anymore!"

An interview can help a student work out what it is that they actually believe.

Philosophy and ethics are deeply personal subjects and cannot be studied effectively without personal engagement with the arguments. Yet as the arguments mount up, students can find themselves at a loss to know what they actually think. It can be helpful to run an interview exercise, with the aim of helping each student work out what they think about the arguments they have been studying. This can be done by the class in the form of peer interviews.

Explain that the point of the interview exercise is simply to elicit information about what the interviewee believes; it isn't meant to be the prelude to a debate. It is often when we talk freely that our ideas start to take shape, so you might give the interviewer a prompt sheet with some questions, and space to note down answers, so that the interviewee is free simply to talk. Alternatively, students could record the interviews on a phone for later transcription.

Questions that can be asked include:

- Can you tell me about some of the views of the philosophers we've discussed?
- Which philosopher do you agree with most?
- Who do you disagree with?
- Can you summarise any of the arguments we've studied?
- Of these arguments, which do you think are the strongest?
- Which are the weakest?
- If I put you on the spot and asked you what you believe and why, what would you say?

Writing philosophy

Part 6

Writing that flows well

"Imagine you are taking your reader on a journey."

It is worth spending some time talking to your students about the qualities of good writing.

Teaching tip

Write a model essay for your students then add comments using the 'Review', 'New Comment' buttons in Word to highlight good stylistic features (and any deliberate errors for correction!).

One of my favourite metaphors is that of the journey of discovery. Ask the class to imagine that they are being driven by a friend on a tour of a new city. What will make the journey enjoyable? What will detract from the pleasure of the experience?

- You'll enjoy the journey more if you feel confident that the driver knows the way.
- It's good to know roughly where you are going before you get there, but a few surprises on the way are nice too.
- Sudden jolts or drastic changes of direction are disconcerting and can distract you from enjoying the view.

With these points in mind, talk about the features of good writing. One important feature is 'smoothness' or 'flow'. There should be a clear sense of continuous, linked, development of ideas. When new topics are introduced, they should be linked to previous material. With this in mind, here are some tips to pass on to students about their writing.

- Start each paragraph with a topic sentence indicating what the paragraph is about.
- Check that the arrangement of your essay or report makes logical sense: are the different sections in a sensible order?
- Look out for bumps or jolts – points where there is a sudden, unexpected change of topic. Think about re-writing these sections by either smoothing them out, re-organising them or editing them out altogether if they are not relevant.

Taking it further

There is an excellent essay writing guide for philosophy students at www.hps.cam.ac.uk/research/wp.html.

ACE essays

"ACE your essays!"

The Argument/Counter-argument/Evaluation model can be used to structure effective philosophy essays.

When providing students with guidance about essay structure, a simple and workable basic model is the ACE pattern:

- Argument
- Counter-argument
- Evaluation.

The ACE model is not meant to provide a structure for a whole essay – for this you will need to talk about what goes into an introduction and a conclusion as well. It is, however, designed to remind students that when they are writing the main section of their essay, they need to consider both sides of the argument and also engage with the arguments. Simply listing points for and against a proposition isn't enough: there needs to be evaluation of the strength of the arguments that are being considered. Evaluation means expressing a judgement about the relative strength of the argument and counter-argument.

For example, an essay on the question 'Is there a God?' might contain a section like this:

- Argument: There must be a God since the universe cannot have come from nothing.
- Counter-argument: If something cannot come from nothing, where did God come from?
- Evaluation: This isn't a good response since God is outside time and doesn't 'come from' anywhere.

Teaching tip

A further merit of this model is that it encourages students to focus their evaluative comments on particular arguments, rather than simply expressing their opinion about the topic as a whole.

Taking it further

By building their essays out of 'ACE' building blocks, students should succeed in covering the ground as well as getting involved in the argument themselves.

The principle of charity

"Now why would someone say a thing like that?"

Asking students to imagine why people say the things they do is a good way of helping them begin to appreciate the strengths of different ideas.

Remind students that they should apply the principle of charity when writing philosophy essays. Before they criticise a position, they should explore what can be said in its defence.

When students have got used to the idea that philosophy involves argument, and therefore criticism of the views of others, they can sometimes fall into the trap of committing the 'straw-man' fallacy. That is, they can attack weak versions of the arguments of those with whom they disagree. At its best, philosophy involves the attempt to think seriously about the grounds for opposing viewpoints and this means giving consideration to the strongest opposing arguments. Students need to be taught the importance of this.

One way of doing this is to tell them about the principle of charity. This principle states that when interpreting what other philosophers say, we should try to find the interpretation which makes their arguments most likely to be true. A simple way of encouraging charitable interpretation is to remind students to 'think inside' the position of the philosopher whose arguments they are considering. This involves asking questions such as:

- What is this philosopher's main aim?
- What are the strengths of their arguments?
- If more than one interpretation of the arguments is possible, which is the strongest?
- Even if the arguments do not prove as much as was hoped, do they still make a good point?

For example, many contemporary philosophers are critical of Descartes' arguments for the claim that the mind is a separate substance to the body. It is worth asking what Descartes' aims were. Part of his aim was to find a way of reconciling belief in the soul with the discoveries of science. Perhaps there are other, better ways of attempting to do this. Furthermore, perhaps Descartes' arguments do establish a weaker form of dualism – a conceptual dualism of ways of thinking, for example, even if they don't prove substance dualism. Perhaps mental and physical terms give us different ways of referring to a single thing.

Taking it further

Ask students to do some research to find examples of charitable and uncharitable critiques of arguments. Then ask them to present the examples they have found. What are the problems with being uncharitable to an opponent? Is it ever justifiable?

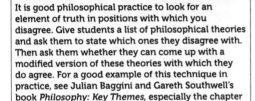

Bonus idea ★

It is good philosophical practice to look for an element of truth in positions with which you disagree. Give students a list of philosophical theories and ask them to state which ones they disagree with. Then ask them whether they can come up with a modified version of these theories with which they do agree. For a good example of this technique in practice, see Julian Baggini and Gareth Southwell's book *Philosophy: Key Themes*, especially the chapter on the philosophy of mind.

SEAL those paragraphs

"Remember this model for paragraphs: State, Explain, Apply, Link."

The SEAL model provides a simple pattern for well-constructed paragraphs.

As well as talking to students about essay construction, it is worth discussing how to construct good paragraphs. A simple, and hopefully memorable, model is as follows:

- State the main point to be made
- Explain the point.
- Apply the point to the question.
- Link to the next paragraph.

One way to illustrate this model is to take a well-written book or article and examine the paragraph construction to see if these elements can be identified. For example, ask students to skim-read the text, looking only at the first sentence in each paragraph. This should illustrate how an author can convey the point to be made in the paragraph in the first line.

Explaining a point may involve spelling out the meaning of a concept by contrasting it with others (see Idea 56). Alternatively it may be a matter of laying out an argument, perhaps formally (see Idea 69).

Emphasise the importance of keeping an essay focused on the question. Asking students to ensure that they apply what they are saying to the question in each paragraph helps them to get into this important habit.

Since good writing flows well, the paragraph should end with a linking sentence. In some cases, the topic sentence of the next paragraph may provide a link (for example, 'So far, we have considered the problems with dualism. Is there anything to be said in its defence?').

The opinion spectrum

"This really helped me develop some arguments of my own."

Students often struggle to identify a position of their own in their essays. One way to help them is to suggest they begin by laying out a spectrum of possible answers.

A good philosophy essay usually consists in a defence of a specific answer to a question. It isn't easy, though, for students to decide which position they will defend. One way of helping them to decide is to use an 'opinion spectrum'. The idea here is that, on many philosophical questions, there is a range of views which can be roughly mapped onto a spectrum. For example, on the mind–body problem, views range between dualism (that the mind is a separate substance to the body) and materialism (that the mind is material), with positions such as non-reductive materialism in the middle.

Aristotle advised that it is a good idea to begin with a survey of the 'endoxa' – the opinions of wise thinkers. This does not mean that only these ideas are true – they might all be wrong. Nor does it imply that it is always right to go for the 'middle-ground' position. But the opinion spectrum can help a student who has no idea what to think. For example, even if the student doesn't know what their view is, they might at least be able to identify views with which they disagree. This can provide a starting point for identifying their own ideas.

Teaching tip

A student might have some idea of what they think but no idea about how to begin laying out arguments. In this case, the opinion spectrum can be useful as a way of identifying positions to argue against.

Developing a line of argument

"Sometimes, attack is the best form of defence."

An effective defence of a philosophical position often begins with a critical analysis of alternative positions.

This idea sounds like a bit of a trick, but it rests on a sound psychological insight. Ask students to think about the best way to go about persuading someone of something in an argument. Is it best to begin with a defence of your own ideas or with a challenge to the other person's position?

Explain that it is best to begin by challenging your opponent's ideas. If people think they already have a satisfactory answer to a question, they won't necessarily be inclined to listen to new ideas. But if they are made aware of problems with their own position, they may be more receptive to new thoughts. Here is a simple model for developing a line of argument:

1. Start with an opinion spectrum, identifying three positions, for example:
   A: God exists.
   B: We don't know whether or not God exists.
   C: God doesn't exist.
Suppose that a student is going to argue for B.

2. State and critically evaluate arguments for A.
3. State and critically evaluate arguments for C.
4. Having challenged A and C, the student should then give arguments in favour of B.
5. The final step is to defend B against objections from positions A and C.

Teaching academic register

"Style matters."

Some simple stylistic guidance can help students improve their philosophy essays.

It is worth spending time with students talking about 'academic register' – or, more simply, how to write clearly and in an appropriate style. Explain to students that academic writing follows rules, or conventions. Just as you wouldn't turn up to a formal occasion like a wedding in casual clothes, so you need your thoughts to be attired in an appropriate fashion. The tone should not be casual or conversational but formal and precise. Here are some pointers:

- Avoid too much use of the first person. It may be appropriate at the start of an essay or report to include a sentence such as 'In this essay, I will argue that ...'. But thereafter, it is best to avoid first personal terms. If 'I think' is being used to express a possibility, replace it with 'Perhaps ...' or 'It is possible that ...'.
- Keep the focus on evidence and argument throughout. Introduce arguments with phrases such as 'It could be argued that ...' or 'There is evidence to suggest that ...', and 'However ...' for counter-arguments. Of course, you can only use these phrases if you do have supporting evidence or arguments – so using phrases such as these can help to keep the focus in the right place.
- When mentioning philosophers, it is conventional to refer to them using surnames (for example, 'Ryle argues that it is a category mistake to treat the mind as a substance.').

Teaching tip

Although it should be obvious, it is also worth reminding students of the importance of correct spelling and grammar throughout their essays.

Taking it further

Give students an example of an essay with poor academic register (preferably not one written by a member of the class) and ask them to work in groups to provide feedback on writing style to the essay-writer.

Signpost sentences

"It's nice to know where you are going."

Signpost sentences throughout an essay help the reader feel comfortable about where things are going.

One of the challenges of writing good philosophy essays is helping the reader find their way through the dense jungle of argument and counter-argument. For this purpose, signpost sentences can be invaluable. The idea is to indicate to the reader where the argument is about to go next, and also to remind them how they reached the present point in the argument. A signpost can provide a reassuring indication that we are still heading in the right direction, and that there is a clear destination in view. They can 'point' in a number of different ways:

- Forward-facing: A sentence which tells the reader what is coming up next. These can either indicate the final destination ('In this essay, I will seek to show that there are good reasons for accepting moral realism.') or the next stage ('First, we will consider the strength of arguments for the fact/value distinction.').
- Retrospective: A sentence summarising the discussion thus far ('We have seen that arguments for the fact/value distinction are unsound.').
- Junctions: These combine retrospective and forward-facing signposts ('Having shown that the main arguments against moral realism fail, I now turn to consider what can be said in favour of this doctrine.') .

Beginning well

"A good introduction draws the reader in."

When helping students to plan their philosophy essays, it is worth spending time talking about the features of a good introduction.

Here is one way to explain the value of a good introduction to students. Ask them to imagine that they are introducing one of their friends to another. What is the point of this social custom of 'the introduction'? Various ideas might be suggested:

- It helps to break the ice.
- It sets the scene for a conversation.
- It establishes common ground and points of mutual interest.

Well, similar points apply when students are writing the introduction to their philosophy essays. The purpose of a good introduction is to draw the reader in, to help prepare them for the rest of the essay and to put them in a receptive frame of mind. More specifically, a good introduction will:

- Persuade the reader that they want to spend time listening to what the writer has to say.
- Set the scene.
- Put up signposts pointing to interesting points to be explored in the essay.
- State what will be argued.

I usually emphasise that introductions should chiefly explore the question that will be answered in the essay.

- What does the question mean?
- What gives rise to the question?
- Why does the question matter?
- In what different ways has the question been answered?
- What answer will be offered in the essay?

Teaching tip

It is occasionally worth asking students to write an introduction to an essay as a homework or class exercise. Once you have checked this, they can go on to the rest of the essay.

Taking it further

Collect some examples of good introductions and not-so-good ones. You could use academic articles, student essays, novels or even textbooks. Ask students to look at these and discuss the way in which they have been written. What good and bad features can they detect? Do they make the reader want to keep reading?

Ending well

"Wrap things up neatly."

A good conclusion reiterates the main points of an essay in a memorable fashion.

Teaching tip

In order to be able to conclude effectively, of course, the student will need to know what the main argument of the essay really is. Sometimes, the fact that they are struggling to conclude may show that they haven't yet got this clear in their own mind, so it may be necessary to go back and do some re-drafting (see Idea 89).

In teaching students how to conclude their essays, remind them of an adage which applies to essay writing as much as it does to oral presentation: say what you are going to say, then say it, then say that you've said it (see Idea 44). Readers might not remember the main arguments of the essay; a good conclusion will help to tie up the threads and reinforce the main points that the essay has sought to establish. Here are some points to explore when helping students write their conclusions:

- A good conclusion should provide a concise summary of the main arguments put forward in the essay.
- It is fine to reiterate points as a way of helping to make them stick in the reader's mind – but don't make the mistake of repeating material from the essay word-for-word.
- Make sure that the conclusion really does sum up the essay – don't include new arguments in the conclusion.

Just as the introduction sets the scene, so it can be appropriate in a conclusion to look at the significance of the essay against a wider backdrop. What further questions have been raised, and what further issues could be explored, if there were more time? These points can be discussed to show that the student is aware of how what they have written relates to the wider philosophical context of the question about which they have written.

Think about the reader

"Don't forget – someone is going to read what you write!"

Asking students to put themselves in the position of someone reading through their essay can help them to spot weaknesses and make improvements.

It is worth pointing out to students that they are writing *for* someone – for themselves, if they will need to re-read the essay during revision, for their teacher, and perhaps for others. Before writing their essay, they should give some thought to the person who will have to read it. Questions that this might prompt include:

- Is the work reasonably laid out on the page?
- Does the language and sentence construction help or hinder the reader? Are there any long, rambling sentences? Would the writing be clearer if the sentences were shorter?
- Does the introduction succeed in setting the scene and drawing the reader in?
- Does each paragraph begin with a topic sentence?
- Have signposts and linking sentences been used in order to help maintain the flow of the argument?
- Is it clear what is going on in each section of the essay? Students may realise that they need to consider argument and counter-argument but then get muddled about which is which. They need to make it really clear which side of the argument is being considered in each paragraph.
- If the essay is being written for a non-expert audience, is the level of language use appropriate? If any technical terms are used, have they been defined?
- Is the use of tenses appropriate? 'In this essay, I will argue' is appropriate; 'I wrote this essay because I thought ...' is not.

Teaching tip

You could introduce this idea by handing students some samples of writing which have been produced for a specific target-audience (for example, advertisements targeting particular age groups). Ask the class to identify the target-audience in each case, then discuss how language has been used appropriately.

Taking it further

An excellent guide to writing philosophy essays can be found here: www.hps.cam.ac.uk/research/wp.html.

Philosophy
projects

Part 7

The power of projects

"This is a chance for you to develop your own ideas."

Project work provides an excellent context for encouraging students to think more deeply and independently about philosophical questions.

Finding ways to encourage and enable students to think for themselves is a constant challenge. In some ways, examinations, which tend to feature short responses to prescribed questions, can discourage the development of skills in independent research and critical thinking. However, project work, whether in the form of qualifications such as the Extended Project, the IB Extended Essay or something similar devised within your own school, has great scope for encouraging students to move further down the road that leads to intellectual independence.

Project work is particularly well-suited to the development of skills in philosophical thinking. Projects can be allocated a period of time ranging from 20 to 80 hours, and during this time students can go on genuine journeys of inquiry. These can take them in a number of directions:

- They could explore an entirely new topic (for example, if their philosophy and ethics course does not include aesthetics, this could be the basis for a project).
- They could use the project to engage in a deeper study of a topic they have encountered in their philosophy and ethics course.
- They could engage in a philosophical study of a topic they have encountered in another subject (looking at the nature of truth in history, for example).

Get the question right

"It's the question that drives the project forward."

Successful projects begin with a clear, focused, manageable question.

Philosophers are often accused of 'only asking questions, and never giving answers'. But when it comes to a philosophy project, the choice of question is absolutely vital. A well-chosen question can open up the path to a successful project, while a poor question can lead to trouble and a project which fails to realise its potential. When students are choosing the title for their philosophy projects:

- Take time to allow the question to crystallise. Most students begin with vague ideas, which gradually become clearer during the initial stages of project work.
- Encourage students to choose questions which genuinely interest them. They will be working on the project for a period of weeks or even months. So it helps if they find it interesting.
- Pick questions that can be researched. There is a body of research literature on most topics in philosophy and ethics. It makes sense to pick a topic that others have written about, since researching their ideas and arguments can provide a natural way into the project.
- Take sides. A good project involves real engagement with the question. Most of the questions of philosophy and ethics are contestable – there is an argument to be had. Rather than allowing students to sit on the fence, encourage them to commit themselves to defending a particular position in the debate. This will lead to greater engagement and it needn't prevent them thinking imaginatively and sympathetically about opposing views.

Teaching tip

The choice of project title is crucial to the success of the project. Allow time for the students to develop ideas, carry out research, then refine their initial thoughts. During this time, your role as a supervisor is to be a critical friend, gently probing to check that their ideas are realistic and achievable.

101

Write as you go

"Don't leave the writing up to the end!"

Successful projects are the result of a continuous developmental process.

This idea is very much an ideal – but it is one worth having. Unless your students are extremely unusual, they will have a tendency to procrastinate, or they may simply be very busy with other work commitments. Either way, there is a temptation to leave writing up the project to the very end of the process. This is not the best strategy for success.

A project is a process, and successful projects usually involve experimentation with ideas, investigation of alternative possibilities and, in most cases, travelling down at least a few blind alleys. All of this makes them extremely beneficial educationally. But this sort of process-based learning can only happen if students commit themselves to working on the project in stages, writing up as they go.

It is much easier for a supervisor to assist a student once something has been written, however basic it is. It can be tempting just to spend time reading – after all, reading is easier than reading plus writing! But the longer students wait before beginning writing, the harder it will be to get started, especially if they see others who have got going well, and begin to feel left behind. So, the golden rule of project work is: write as you go!

Supervisory logs

"It helps to have a record of what I said to a student when we last met – especially if targets were agreed!"

A supervisory log is a helpful tool for monitoring progress with project work.

The role of a project supervisor is to keep students moving steadily forwards with their project work. A supervisory log can be really helpful here. It can be difficult, from week to week, to remember what was said to individual students, particularly if you are in charge of a large group. Noting down agreed targets means that you have a point from which to begin the next tutorial. I have a colleague who likes to remind students that they 'made that excuse last week'! Here are a few pointers about log keeping:

- Experiment with different formats. A simple method is to have a file with a page for each student – this is a bit like a file of consultant's notes. With file in hand, ask students how they are getting on and what problems they face, and scribble down notes as they talk. While you're writing, you can begin to think of things to say to help them forwards.
- An online record can be useful. Keep a spreadsheet with a row for each student, with a column for their research question (even the students can forget what question they are actually working on!), and a note of any special educational needs. Each week make a brief entry recording progress and targets. Often there may not be much to write, but occasionally – say, after you've read a draft of their work – you'll have some detailed points. Write these in your log then email a copy of the guidance to the student.

Journals for meta-cognition

"Tell the story of your journey of ideas."

A student journal adds an extra dimension to project work and can help students develop higher-order thinking skills.

Since a project is a process, it makes sense to ask students to keep a record of how things are going. A journal that is updated on a regular basis can provide a good 'back-story' to a project. It provides a space in which students can explore ideas which may or may not see the light of day in the finished project. More importantly, perhaps, it provides an opportunity for them to reflect on the progress of their work and to explore possible solutions to the challenges they face.

Emphasise to students that their journal should be more than a simple record of activities. While it is important to keep track of what has been done in terms of research and the development of argument, the really important elements in journals are the reflective elements: the entries in which they explore the intellectual challenges they face, as they seek to explore philosophical and ethical ideas, and develop their own response to what they are researching. In this way, writing a journal becomes an exercise in 'thinking about thinking' – it is a chance to develop those all-important meta-cognitive skills. Here are some points of advice to give students:

- Writing a journal is a chance to reflect on how your project is going, as well as to record what you have achieved so far.
- Write down what you have been thinking about, and what you are feeling, as well as what you have actually done.

- The decisions you make about your project are important. Use your journal to explore these decisions. What options are open to you at any point? Why have you decided to go one way rather than another?
- Most projects run into problems at some point. Write about these. When the problems have been solved, write about what you've learnt during the problem-solving process.

In my experience, when writing journals, students tend to focus on describing their activities rather than reflecting on their thought-processes. They will need encouragement from their supervisor to write reflectively. They may also need to be reminded that the journal is not a diary: the purpose is to provide a record of progress with their project, not to give an account of the details of their personal life.

Taking it further

An obvious extension to the idea of a written journal is a blog. You might want to set up a system for students to write blog entries about their project work.

Thematic or chronological?

"Tell me the story."

Writing research up as a narrative helps to make it easier to read and means that students have to work at synthesising their sources.

Teaching tip

There are different views about the value of Wikipedia as a research source for student projects. One area where it really can help is in mapping out the areas that will be researched in a project. Many topics that students choose to write about have Wikipedia pages, and these pages have tables of contents which can be a very helpful starting point for students who are planning their research.

In Idea 51, I referred to research as a two-stage process. After the collection of source materials comes the writing-up stage. I recommend to students that instead of just writing about their sources, one at a time, they think about how they can link them together. One good way of organising their research is to cast it in the form of a narrative, in which they trace out developments chronologically. Alternatively, they might choose to structure their research by investigating a range of themes relating to their topic.

It is a good idea to make the decision about how the research will be laid out while the research process is still going on. This means that further work can readily be 'slotted into' the structure.

So, for example, suppose a student is writing a project on the ethics of euthanasia. They might choose to organise this into:

- Types of euthanasia
- The history of attitudes towards euthanasia
- Religious and ethical arguments for and against
- Legal issues.

Within each of these thematic areas, there will probably be a story to tell about the developments that led up to the present day. Encouraging students to write in this way helps them to develop their skills in analysis and synthesis of sources.

Description to evaluation

"First find out what other people think – then get stuck into the argument for yourself."

It is a good idea to tell students to create separate research and discussion sections in their projects.

When it comes to writing philosophy and ethics projects, students tend to be much more comfortable researching what other people think than creating and defending their own arguments. Creating your own arguments is challenging; it calls for the higher-order thinking skills of critical reflection and evaluation.

As a result, many student projects are dominated by reviews of other people's ideas and arguments, with perhaps a little commentary of their own. The student may only venture to give their own views in the conclusion, by which stage it is too late for there to be much engagement in argument.

To avoid this, explain to students that it is almost always a good idea to create separate 'research' and 'discussion' sections. The research section should provide an outline of the background to the topic. In the discussion section, the student can join in the argument, drawing on source materials to defend their own point of view and to find counter-arguments which need to be addressed.

A good way of explaining this distinction is to refer to a court of law. In trials, the first stage is the gathering of evidence from witnesses. Once all the evidence is in, the lawyers will use it to build arguments for either the prosecution or the defence. In the same way, the first stage of a research project is the gathering of evidence, this can then be used in the discussion section to build a case.

Taking it further

Once students understand the difference between the research and discussion sections of a project, you can explore the appropriate style of writing to be used in each. As a rule, the research section should be written in a more objective, neutral style (for example, 'Sources state that ...'). Once the discussion begins, however, it is time for the student to engage in the argument and there will be more use of first-person language (for example, 'I will argue ...').

Do it again!

"That's a good first draft – now for the second!"

Project work provides an excellent opportunity for students to learn to improve their writing through re-drafting.

Like any craft, writing involves a fair bit of going over and over the same material in order to smooth out the wrinkles, soften any rough edges and apply some polish. In many student assignments, work is handed in, marked, and that is it. But with project work, done over a period of weeks or months, there is a chance to improve work through re-drafting. This can be a valuable part of the process. Here are some pointers and questions to use when checking drafts:

- Set a series of deadlines for sections of the project for example: first draft of research, first draft of discussion, first draft of entire project. These can help to motivate students to get writing – and really, there is little a supervisor can do until they have some work on which to comment.
- When checking research sections, check that the work is indeed the student's own (typing a few sentences into a search engine usually works).
- Assess whether the work is balanced – have all aspects been covered?
- Could the writing be tightened up?
- Is the student wandering off-topic?
- Have they included citations?
- In the discussion section, are they considering argument and counter-argument?
- Are the different sections linked together so that the text flows smoothly?

Work in progress

"Now it's your turn to tell us about your project."

A work in progress seminar is a chance for you to check on student's progress and for them to develop their oral presentation skills.

After a few weeks of project work, holding a 'work in progress' seminar can provide an enjoyable and rewarding opportunity for students to present their work to the class.

This does not have to involve preparing a big ten-minute presentation. It may involve no more than pulling the group together during the second half of a lesson and asking each student to talk for a few minutes about their research.

You might want to warn the class in advance, not least because knowing that they are going to have to present their work can act as an incentive to crack on with it, since they won't want to be embarrassed into admitting that they have nothing to report!

You will probably need to remind students that others in the group don't know what their question is, so they will need to explain this at the outset.

Once they have spoken for a few minutes, be ready with some questions. These can be general ones (for example, 'What has been your most useful source so far?', 'Which side of the argument are you on?'), or more specific questions arising from what they have said.

> **Teaching tip**
>
> It is worth allowing time for the group to respond as well, with questions or comments. Sometimes, these discussions can turn into really interesting explorations of the topic, which can be stimulating both for the presenter and the rest of the class.

Well-presented projects

"Now it's time to make it look really smart."

A few simple changes can do a lot to improve the quality of presentation of a project.

First impressions count, and the first impression that a project makes will depend a great deal on how much work has gone into making it look good on the page. Paying attention to things like font, spacing, headings and tables of contents can do a lot to make a project look like it is worth reading. Here are some tips:

- Don't use single spacing (too narrow) or double-spacing (too wide). I think 1.15 spacing works well. To create this in Word, select the whole document, go to Paragraph, Line Spacing, Multiple, 1.15.
- Use the Styles bar to change the style of your headings. Click on a heading, and style it by clicking on the Heading 1 button (for main headings) and Heading 2 (for sub-headings). This will change the font of your headings. You can do the same for the title.
- Now experiment with the 'Change styles' button. If you drag the mouse over the 'Style Set' option you will find a range of different styles. Selecting one can instantly change the appearance of the entire document. I like 'Distinctive', but 'Manuscript' might work best for a project report.
- After the title page, insert a blank page. Go to the 'References' button on the toolbar, then click on 'Table of Contents' and select one of the Automatic Tables. This will pick up all the headings in your document, together with their page numbers.

Beyond the philosophy classroom

Part 8

Running a philosophy club

"I really enjoy meeting after school to talk philosophy."

A philosophy club offers a space for students to explore philosophy for themselves, in the company of others who share their interest.

Running a philosophy club is a good idea if you want to nurture the interest and enthusiasm of students for the subject. A philosophy club may meet for around half an hour during a lunch break, or after school. In my experience, these sessions offer a tremendous way for students to explore philosophical ideas with greater freedom than the classroom setting allows. Here are some pointers for setting up and running a philosophy club:

- The club will rely on the enthusiasm of a few dedicated members. While some people will drop in occasionally, you need to nurture a 'nucleus' of students who will help to keep the club running.
- Appoint students to positions of responsibility. For example, one or two students can take on the post of 'Secretary' and help to run the club (putting up posters, keeping records of meetings, choosing topics for discussion).
- There are various ways of structuring meetings. To start with, you might select a theme and choose some suitable stimulus material. As they grow in confidence, you can allow students themselves to select topics and begin the discussion.
- Food and drink are always welcome!

Taking it further

I once ran a club for students in Years 10 and 11. Each week, the students met to discuss a thought experiment from Julian Baggini's book *The Pig that Wants to be Eaten*. These discussions generated a lot of excitement and we carried on through an email group once the sessions were finished.

Visiting speakers

"That talk gave me a lot to think about!"

Asking a philosopher to visit school to give a guest lecture is a good way of stretching students.

I find that inviting philosophers into school to give a guest talk can be rewarding for everyone. There are many philosophers who are only too glad to receive invitations to share their ideas with a young, enthusiastic audience. For students, a guest talk can provide an insight into, for example, what it might be like to encounter philosophy at university. Here are some ideas for visiting speakers:

- The Royal Institute of Philosophy runs a scheme called 'Philosophy in Schools' (details here: www.royalinstitutephilosophy.org/funding-education/philosophy-in-schools).
- The charity 'Speakers for Schools' offers free talks for schools and has a number of philosophers in its list (www.speakers4schools.org) .
- You could contact a local university to see if they would be willing to send a speaker.

As a rule, it is a good idea to invite speakers who you know will communicate well to students of school age. Some philosophers are better than other at this! Go by recommendation, or invite philosophers you yourself have heard speak.

Make sure you brief the speaker carefully about an appropriate length of talk, the background knowledge of the audience and the format for any discussion, either during or after the talk.

Ideally, guest talks should be pitched at a level which makes them accessible but challenging.

Teaching tip

Often, the very best events happen when speakers invite questions and discussion during their talk, turning it into an interactive philosophical exploration. When you are briefing the speaker, ask them whether they prefer to take questions at the end or to allow interaction during their talk. Bear in mind that the potential for effective interaction can vary depending on the size and maturity of the audience.

Powerful presentations

"I understood things much better once I'd had to present to the group."

Asking students to give an oral presentation is a good way of helping them think through a philosophical issue.

There are many good reasons for inviting students to give oral presentations: they gain valuable skills, their confidence can grow and it gives them an opportunity to air their own ideas. Presentations can be particularly helpful when students are learning philosophy and ethics, because thinking about how best to present a topic can help students to understand it more fully.

I encourage all my students who have written philosophy and ethics projects to give an oral presentation of these towards the end of the course. Working on their presentations helps them to think through the logic of the arguments they have studied, and the relationship between different theories.

When it comes to the actual presentation, I remind students of one of the golden rules of oral presentation: 'less is more' (see Idea 44 for more points about general presentation skills). When preparing a presentation based on a project, I usually recommend a time limit of ten minutes. I point out that it will only be possible to cover the elements of their project: the main findings from their research, and some points about the central line of argument. It is also worth reminding students that they may well know much more about their chosen topic than their audience, so they will have to think about how to convey their ideas simply and accessibly.

A philosophy VLE

"Online discussion is a terrific format for philosophical debate."

A philosophy virtual learning environment (VLE) is a powerful tool for enabling students to develop their skills in reasoning and debate.

Students may be more willing to post their thoughts in response to a stimulus piece than to take part in face-to-face discussion. The fact that they are writing their thoughts out is significant too: it allows them to compose arguments more carefully than they would if they were talking. Another advantage of using an online platform is that they have a chance to read and then respond to what others have written. Threads can grow over a period of time. Here are some tips:

- When getting a thread started, it is a good idea to write a short piece of stimulus text, and perhaps include a link to a video or podcast. You might want to record yourself and a colleague discussing a philosophical problem, as a way of setting the scene for the students.
- As with face-to-face discussions, pick topics which are likely to generate discussion and debate. Ethical questions work very well, as do questions from the philosophy of religion, or topics such as personal identity. Questions from metaphysics (for example, What is time?) can also prove stimulating.
- As well as threads that you start, you might well want a space on your VLE for students to start discussions. For example, if they are working on philosophy and ethics projects, create a space where project students can write about their topic and interact with their peers.

Teaching tip

Populate your VLE with links to useful resources. See idea 100 for some suggestions. You can also ask students to recommend useful sites they have found.

Running online discussions

"Philosophical discussion isn't just about sounding off!"

Effective online discussion needs gentle but firm moderation.

Thanks to social media, most students can be quite articulate when it comes to posting their thoughts online. However, there is a big difference between the unstructured, unfocused chat that they might engage in with online friends and formal discussion of philosophical arguments. Getting the right balance of freedom and structure is important.

Surprisingly, students often interact quite fluently online, even when their peers are in the same room! It might seem strange to invite a group of students to converse online, when they could talk face-to-face, but there are advantages. As mentioned in Idea 95, they can compose their arguments better when writing. They can respond to earlier posts, or bring in weblinks to enrich the discussion. You can also make arrangements for 'group posting', so that students who are nervous about writing as an individual can nevertheless still contribute as part of a small group.

One important point to consider is the way you interact online with the students. When a teacher posts, it can have an effect on the conversation that you don't want. Students might be reluctant to argue against you, for example. I tend to hold back and post only if I think that the student I'm replying to will be confident enough to reply back.

The other thing that threads need is some moderation and occasional editing! A philosophical conversation can be free-flowing and inventive but you do want it to stay on topic. Be prepared to delete silly or distracting remarks.

Philosophy café

"Food, drink and philosophy go well together."

Creating a café atmosphere can encourage more open, reflective, meaningful discussion.

From Socrates in the market place of Athens, to Jean-Paul Sartre in Les Deux Magots, philosophers have carried out their enquiries into the meaning of life in public spaces. There is something appropriate about the café setting: a café is a place for conversation, and what is philosophy, if not a great, continued conversation about the ideas which shape our lives? Where possible, then, I think it is a great idea to carry on philosophical discussion over a coffee or a cola.

The great advantage of discussions held in the social, informal setting of a café (or even over lunch during a school day) is that the setting positively encourages you to explore the fascinating points at which life and philosophy overlap. I have had fascinating philosophical conversations with students over lunch, on topics ranging from the profound (the existence of God, or the possibility of knowledge) to the trivial (such as the definition of 'sandwich').

When the discussion happens in such contexts, the formalities of the classroom can be forgotten and this means that it is possible for you to explore philosophical questions in a more personal, meaningful way. Somehow it feels more appropriate to talk about your personal beliefs in such settings.

Teaching tip

If you are running a philosophy club (Idea 92) it is a great idea to include food and drink. You may not be able to go as far as having a sit-down meal, but even if you just provide soft drinks and biscuits, you will help to create the conditions for students to relax, converse, and, hopefully, mull over some philosophical topics as they enjoy the refreshments.

Philosophical drop-in

"Philosophical questioning can happen in more or less any subject area."

There is value in dropping-in on other subjects to spend some time exploring the philosophical questions they raise.

Teaching tip

Philosophy is a terrific catalyst of independent thought. Just like a catalyst, you don't necessarily need huge amounts to start a reaction. When planning a programme of drop-in lessons, you don't need to do more than one or two per term. Even a brief encounter with philosophy can have surprising results.

One of the great joys of philosophical investigations is that they can begin from more or less any subject area. So as well as teaching classes in philosophy and ethics, it is a good idea, occasionally, to drop-in on other subjects, and spend some time exploring philosophical ideas in this context.

In a science class, you could explore questions such as 'What is scientific truth?' or 'What is the difference between a fact and a theory?' (the Eleusis game works well here – see Idea 13).

In a maths lesson you could ask 'What is a number?' or 'Can a period of space be infinitely divided?' (this links to Zeno's Paradox, discussed in Idea 17).

In an English lesson, questions such as 'What is meaning?' or 'Is there such a thing as the true interpretation of a text?' are worth discussion.

History is a great context for exploring epistemology, with questions such as 'What is a fact?' and 'If there is no evidence of past events, are there still truths about them?'.

It takes some organisation to make these lessons work. Some negotiation with colleagues will be necessary and you will need to explain to both teachers and students what the point of the lesson is. Students really do enjoy the opportunity to take a break from 'normal' learning and to ask some of the deeper, philosophical questions that are raised by the subjects they are studying.

Run a teachers' philosophy group

"Meeting to discuss philosophy with colleagues helps me to keep going."

A philosophy group for teachers can be a source of inspiration and refreshment.

At the school where I teach, a number of teachers with interests in philosophy like to meet, once a term usually, to discuss philosophy. The group is made up of teachers with different subject specialisms, but what we share is a love of philosophical discussion. The main point of meeting is simply to enjoy talking philosophy together (and, it should be said, to enjoy some good wine and food!). But one of the benefits of meeting in this way is that it can help you to return, refreshed, to the classroom. As a teacher, you are constantly 'giving out', and a philosophy group can be a place to come and 're-charge': to re-connect with the thing that makes you want to teach philosophy, namely the sheer delight of exploring the deepest questions of all.

The best discussions happen when there is some clear initial focal point. Usually, we agree to read a book, or, if time is short, an article. This gives us something from which to begin, and, almost inevitably, as the evening wears on, the discussion ranges wider. I don't expect discussion like this would ever count as formal CPD, but it certainly can be very instructive for all concerned, particularly when insights from different subjects are brought into the conversation. So – why not take the plunge and invite a few colleagues to join you in forming a teachers' philosophy group?

Taking it further

Once your group is up and running, you can take it in turns to recommend readings and introduce new themes. This way, colleagues can choose philosophical stimulus material which makes links to their own subject area.

Philosophical inspirations

"There is so much good stuff out there on the internet!"

The best philosophy websites are accessible, interesting and inspiring.

Teaching tip

Create a group email list for your class. When you find a good new philosophical website, share the link with them straightaway.

By way of finale, here are some of my favourite philosophy websites.

The Institute of Arts and Ideas (www.iai.tv)
This contains some highly stimulating discussions and debates, with helpful 'Jump in' boxes to allow you to access specific topics.

Microphilosophy (www.microphilosophy. net)
Julian Baggini has a wonderful style. He articulates philosophical ideas in a stimulating, accessible manner and his discussions, videos and podcasts range over all sorts of fascinating topics.

Philosophy Bites (www.philosophybites.com)
Nigel Warburton and David Edmonds have compiled an enormous number of interviews with world-leading philosophers. The quality of discussion and range of topics make this a terrific classroom resource.

Closer to Truth (www.closertotruth.com)
Robert Lawrence Kuhn has also interviewed an extraordinarily wide range of philosophers, scientists and theologians. The clips on his website are helpfully indexed and are an ideal length for use as discussion starters in the classroom.

Philosophy Talk (www.philosophytalk.org)
John Perry and Ken Taylor broadcast entertaining weekly podcasts on philosophical questions.

Taking it further

If you haven't joined Twitter, it is worth doing so, even if you don't want to tweet. Following a few philosophers or teachers is an easy way of picking up more tips for great resources.